Anonymous

Valparaiso, Indiana City Directory

Anonymous

Valparaiso, Indiana City Directory

ISBN/EAN: 9783337088811

Printed in Europe, USA, Canada, Australia, Japan

Cover: Foto ©Suzi / pixelio.de

More available books at **www.hansebooks.com**

FOR RELIABLE WORK, TURNED OUT ON
SHORT NOTICE, GO TO

L. W. BLOCH'S

Steam  Laundry

40 West Main Street,

VALPARAISO, - INDIANA.

MENDING SATISFACTORILY ATTENDED
TO WITHOUT CHARGE.

VALPARAISO

PORTER COUNTY, IND.

CITY DIRECTORY

1893

CONTAINING A COMPLETE LIST

OF

RESIDENTS, CITY AND COUNTY OFFICIALS, POLICE AND FIRE
DEPARTMENTS, CHURCHES AND SOCIETIES AND
THEIR OFFICERS;

ALSO

VALUABLE INFORMATION RELATING TO RATES OF POSTAGE, POSTOFFICE MONEY
ORDERS, ARRIVAL AND DEPARTURE OF MAILS, ETC.

PUBLISHED ANNUALLY.

PRICE, 50 CENTS.

COPYRIGHTED.
KRAFT & RADCLIFFE,
Publishers of City Directories,
CHICAGO.

VALPARAISO CITY DIRECTORY.

22d YEAR.

THE MESSENGER

E. ZIMMERMAN, Editor and Prop.

Published every Thursday, at $1.50 per annum, six months, 75 cents, four months, 50 cents.

IN ADVANCE.

The Best Advertising Medium.   General News of State at Large.
Contains all the Local News.   General News of Public Interest.
A Home Paper of High Standard.

SUBSCRIBE FOR THE MESSENGER NOW AND KEEP POSTED ON CURRENT EVENTS.

DAILY SUN

$4.00 PER YEAR.   2D YEAR.   10C. PER WEEK.

The • Job • Printing • Department

IS FURNISHED WITH

NEW AND BEST DISPLAY TYPE,

To do all kinds of Printing, in the best style of the Art, promptly and at fair rates.   Give us a call.

MESSENGER BUILDING,

SOUTHEAST CORNER
WASHINGTON AND JEFFERSON STREETS,   VALPARAISO, IND.

Grand Central Hotel

ED. A. MEE,
Proprietor.

RATES $2.00 PER DAY.

OFFICE, DINING AND SAMPLE ROOMS ON FIRST FLOOR.

23 West Main Street,   VALPARAISO, IND.

Henderlong Bros. & Kirk

MANUFACTURERS AND DEALERS IN

Sash, Doors, Blinds, Screens, Mouldings, Trimmings, Lumber,
Lath, Shingles, Brackets and Builders' Hardware.
Round and Square Tanks, Etc.

WE MAKE A SPECIALTY OF EMBOSSED INTERIOR FINISH.

OFFICE AND FACTORY, 83 CHICAGO STREET, COR. WESTON

Introductory

The publishers of THE VALPARAISO CITY DIRECTORY for 1893 have spared no labor or expense in securing full data for a complete, correct and reliable reference directory. Every residence, manufacturing and business house inside the corporation limits has been carefully canvassed by expert census takers, and no effort has been withheld to secure the name of every adult to classify in its proper place in our pages.

The population of Valparaiso has evidently increased very much since the official census was taken, or the city did not receive due credit at that time for what inhabitants it really had. We have the names in our columns which, according to expert figures, give Valparaiso a population of 6,660. This figure is quite conservative and does not include the students at the Normal School. Adding then the average attendance at that institution of 1,900, we have a total population of 8,560.

All information of a valuable character has been sought for insertion in this work. Every society, church and other organization, has been solicited for information as to the particulars of their location, officers, time and place of meeting, etc., and as far as the publishers know the lists are complete.

We wish to thank the city officials, the press, and the many citizens of Valparaiso, who have aided us in our efforts, and trust that the result of our labors will be appreciated.

Very respectfully,

KRAFT & RADCLIFFE.

THE DAILY STAR

J. A. McCONAHY, Editor and Proprietor.

The Star is now in its fifth year; issued every evening (except Sunday), and is one of the spiciest sheets published in the State, teeming with well written

 LOCALS AND GENERAL NEWS.

THE WEEKLY STAR

PUBLISHED EVERY WEDNESEAY AT $1.00 A YEAR.

JOB PRINTING NEATLY AND PROMPTLY DONE

Office under First Nation. Bank.

12 S. WASHINGTON ST.   VAL ARAISO, IND.

SCHOOL THE ENTIRE YEAR. STUDENTS MAY ENTER AT ANY TIME AND SELECT THEIR OWN STUDIES.

NORTHERN INDIANA NORMAL SCHOOL

and Business Institute

VALPARAISO, IND.

The LARGEST and BEST EQUIPPED NORMAL SCHOOL
IN THE UNITED STATES.

DEPARTMENTS.—Preparatory, Teachers (including Kindergarten Work, Teachers Training Class and Pedagogy), Collegiate (including Scientific, Classic and Select Courses), Special Science, Civil Engineering, Pharmacy, Commercial, Music, Fine Art, Phonography and Typewriting, Telegraphic and Review. Each department is a school within itself, yet all, with the exception of private lessons in Music, are INCLUDED IN ONE TUITION.

Specialists as Instructors are Provided for each Department.
Though the attendance is large yet the classes are sectioned so as to contain, on an average, not to exceed 50 students.

THE COMMERCIAL DEPARTMENT in connection with the school is everywhere acknowledged to be the most complete Commercial College in the land. It is supplied with the most extensive line of offices ever attempted by any Business School.

NO OTHER INSTITUTION OF LEARNING OFFERS FOR ONE TUITION ANYTHING LIKE AS MANY SUBJECTS FROM WHICH TO SELECT.

The best evidence that the work is satisfactory is the constantly increasing demand for those trained here. *Expenses less than at any other place.*

Tuition $10 per term. Board and furnished room, $1.50 to $1 90 per week. Catalogue mailed free.   Address

H. B. BROWN, Principal, or O. P. KINSEY, Associate.

GO TO

HESS & HOYT

FOR Fine Bakery Goods

FIRST-CLASS RESTAURANT.

CIGARS AND CONFECTIONERY.

22 East Main Street.   VALPARAISO, IND.

LUMBER AND COAL

WHITE, McFETRICH & CO.

80 West Mechanic Street,
NEAR FT. WAYNE DEPOT,

VALPARAISO, IND.

Pine Lumber, Shingles, Sash, Doors, Windows, Etc.

HARD AND SOFT COAL AND SMITHING COAL

PORTER COUNTY COURT HOUSE

VALPARAISO CITY DIRECTORY.

NO. 1.   VOL. L.   WHOLE NO. 2683.

Porter County Vidette

TALCOTT & WELTY, Proprietors.

PUBLISHED EVERY THURSDAY
$1.50 PER YEAR, IN ADVANCE.

The Largest Circulation
The Best Advertising Medium
The Newest and Spiciest Newspaper
The Most Local and General News
AND WITHAL The Paper "Par Excellence" for our Citizens

Bring or send in your Subscriptions
Send in or bring in your Advertisements
You shall be Faithfully Served

JOB PRINTING

OF ALL KINDS, IN THE LATEST STYLE TYPES, AT LOWEST RATES.

ONLY CALL AND SEE US.

16 South Lafayette Street

VALPARAISO, IND.

W. C. TALCOTT, EDITOR.
E. WELTY, MANAGER.

J. W. TRUMAN,
MERCHANT TAILOR

ACADEMY OF MUSIC BLOCK,

Main and Washington Streets, VALPARAISO.

BLOOD & LINDNER,

MANUFACTURERS OF BEST BRANDS OF

 ## FLOUR and FEED

AT THE SAGER MILLS.

Store, Corner Mechanic and South Washington Sts.

VALPARAISO, IND.

WILLIAM M. McKENZIE
Hack and Baggage Line

PASSENGERS AND BAGGAGE TAKEN
TO AND FROM DEPOTS, ETC.

Leave Orders at Felton's Livery Barn.

RESIDENCE, 75 MECHANIC ST.   MAIN STREET, COR. MICHIGAN.

L. M. PIERCE
Insurance

Leading Companies in Fire, Live Stock and Life Insurance.

LOSSES PROMPTLY PAID

12 South Washington St.   VALPARAISO, IND.

VALPARAISO U. S. POST OFFICE.

MARK L. DeMOTTE, Postmaster.
MARK L. DICKOVER, Ass't Postmaster.

BEN. F. SMITH, Mailing Clerk.
GOLDIE C. BENNY, Gen'l Delivery Clerk.

WALLACE ROCKWELL,
JAMES J. GRAY,   } Carriers.
JOHN H. ARNOLD,

MAILS ARRIVE.

FROM THE EAST.		FROM THE WEST.	
5:12 a. m.	3:34 p. m.	1:22 a. m.	4:40 p. m.
5:45 "	5:57 "	8:55 "	6:45 "
10:20 "	8:15 "	9:46 "	10:30 "
2:45 p. m.		11:00 "	

MAILS CLOSE.

GOING EAST.		GOING WEST.	
8:30 a. m.	4:15 p. m.	9:45 a. m.	5:25 p. m.
9:20 "	6:20 "	2:25 p. m.	7:45 "
10:35 "	7:45 "	3:00 "	

Mails are open usually about 30 minutes after arrival of trains.

POSTAGE RATES.

First Class.—Letters and sealed matter generally 2 cents per ounce or fraction of an ounce. Drop letters 2 cents where there is free delivery, otherwise 1 cent.

Second Class.—Newspapers and Periodicals mailed by publisher 1 cent per pound or fraction thereof.

Third Class.—Books, Circulars and Printed Matter generally, if unsealed, 1 cent for two ounces or fraction thereof. Newspapers and Magazines 1 cent for four ounces or fraction thereof.

Fourth Class.—Merchandise unsealed and containing no writing 1 cent for an ounce or fraction thereof.

Postal Cards, three sizes, 1 cent each.

Postal Cards, with prepaid reply, 2 cents.

Postage Stamps are issued in the following denominations: 1, 2, 3, 4, 5, 6, 10, 15, 30 and 90 cents.

Postage stamps are not legal tender.

Postmasters are not allowed to exchange one denomination for another.

WEIGHT.

Unsealed mail packages are limited to four pounds each, except single books, for which there is no limit, nor is the weight limited on sealed packages paid at letter rates. The standard pound is avoirdupois, 16 ounces.

The standard or unit of weight on which the postage rate is made is for first-class matter, one ounce; second class, one pound; third class (except newspapers), two ounces; fourth class, one ounce. Transient newspapers and periodicals, four ounces.

JOHN H. RADER,

DEALER IN

Dry Goods, Groceries and Tinware

CONFECTIONERY AND NOTIONS.
CASH PAID FOR BUTTER AND EGGS.

83 East Erie Street.   VALPARAISO, IND.

T. B. LOUDERBACK,

Carriage and Wagon Manufacturer

DOES A GENERAL BLACKSMITHING BUSINESS.

Special Attention to Repairing and Painting.

JUSTICE OF THE PEACE.

Office, 61 E. Main St.
Residence, 91 E. Main St.   VALPARAISO, IND.

HARBECK & ROGERS,

MANUFACTURERS OF

CHURCH AND LODGE

Furniture

PULPITS, CONFESSIONALS,
BAPTISMAL FONTS.
ALTARS, CHAIRS, Etc.

Also, Re-upholstering and Repairing of every description in a superior manner.

South Lafayette St.

NEAR MAIN.

R. P. WOLFE,

AGENT FOR

Chicago Suit and Pants Co.

Suits to Order, $16 to $40.
Pants, $4.00 and upwards.

First-class Fit Guaranteed in Every Case.

ALWAYS A FASHIONABLE LINE OF

Foreign and Domestic Suitings on hand.

Sample Room at Express Office,

VALPARAISO, IND.

VALPARAISO CITY DIRECTORY.

E. V. ARNOLD,

THE BEST

Undertaker, Embalmer and Funeral Director

FIRST DOOR SOUTH OF PRESBYTERIAN CHURCH

VALPARAISO, IND.

Residence, 68 N. Michigan St.

WM. JOHNSTON,
JNO. WARE,   DIRECTORS WM. E. PINNEY,
L. R. SKINNER,   S. P. CORBOY,
                        J. H. SKINNER.

State Bank of Valparaiso

WM. E. PINNEY, Prest.   TRANSACTS A
JNO. WARE, Vice-Prest. GENERAL BANK-
J. H. SKINNER, Cashier. ING BUSINESS.

J. W. SIEB, Live Stock

FRESH AND SMOKED MEATS.

Franklin St.,
East Side Public Square.   VALPARAISO, IND.

"COURT" JOHN REDDINGTON, Proprietor.

FINEST LINE OF

LIQUORS & CIGARS

No. 16 South Washington Street,   VALPARAISO.

SUGGESTIONS TO THE PUBLIC.

1. Address mail matter legibly and fully. Give name of Postoffice and State in full, street and house number, or box number. If the office be a small one add name of the county.
2. Put your name and address upon upper left hand corner of all matter mailed by you.
3. On foreign letters always place the name of the country in full.
4. Do not use thin envelopes. Stamped envelopes are the best.
5. Register all valuable letters.
6. Send money by money order.
7. If your mail is delivered by carrier provide a letter-box at your residence or place of business.
8. Affix stamps securely and on upper right hand corner.
9. Do not tender for postage stamps money so mutilated as to be incurrent, or more than twenty-five cents in copper or nickel coins.
10. Do not ask the postmaster or clerks to affix stamps for you.
11. Do not ask credit for postage stamps.
12. Do not ask credit for money-orders.
13. Do not tender checks or drafts in payment of money-orders, or any money except that which is legal tender and National bank notes.
14. Upon the corner of envelopes supplied by hotels, direct what disposal shall be made of letters undelivered.

CITY OFFICERS.

FRANK P. JONES, Mayor,   S. ROSS MARTIN, Clerk.
GEORGE SCHWARZKOPF, Treasurer.   W. C. SERGEANT, Marshal.

COUNCILMEN.—J. H. Patrick, E. W. Dille, D. E. Simons, Freeman Crosby, Henry Binnamon, Fred. Shoemaker, S. P. Corboy and V. H. Wendt.

FIRE DEPARTMENT.—L. T. White, chief; Wm. H. Newland, assistant chief. *Hook and Ladder Co. No. 1.*—J. C. Rock, G. W. Crouse, A. F. Winslow, James Adams, David Barry, C. L. Dille, D. F. Winslow, E. L. James, S. Ramsey, D. J. Smith, Chas. Stoner, Wilford Trudell, Ed. Gregory, Benj. Fleming, H. Fleming, C. Herrick, S. Dillingham, A. L. Collins, L. L. Merton, A. L. Pierce, Ed. Brown, John Fleming, Roy Pierce. *Hose Co. No. 1.*—E. T. Chester, Marion Breyfogle, F. A. Lepell, Wm. Edwards, James Burke, A. B. Lepell, Wm. Lederer, Frank Faley, Don G. Lytle, John Broon.huff, Henry Sayles, J. T. Massey, V. H. Wendt, Geo. W. Billings, Joseph Sego, James Griswold, Joe Adams. *Hose Co. Alert or No. 2.*—W. H. Newland, W. J. Henry, George Fox, John Vantreese, Joseph L. Doyle, E. E. Cunningham, J. A. McNay, J. W. Halladay, W. H. Gardner, Ed. Skinner, Wm. Mahaffey, Fred. Shoemaker, H. W. Dye. *Hose Co. No. 3*—Bert Wise, Wm. Thum, Albert Thum, Wm. Barber, J. M. Salisbury, E. C. Bowser, Grant Wade, W. Blade, Myron Brown, Frank Card, George Card, Will Wasser, Ed. Truesdell, Hale Allen, Lon Jones, Rillis Winegar, August Jackmore, R. A. Heritage.

CITY COMMISSIONERS—Wm. E. Pinney, Robt. P. Jones, James Leonard, George Finney, Peter Schultz.

CITY BOARD OF HEALTH.—W. L. Reading, president; Dr. A. P. Letherman, secretary, John Van Treese and Aaron Parks. Meets at call of secretary at his office.

COUNTY OFFICERS.

John S. Gillette, judge of circuit court; Willis C. McMahan, prosecuting attorney; Wm. H. Dowdell, assistant prosecuting attorney; E. C. O'Neill, clerk; G. S. Bartholomew, deputy clerk; Joseph Sego, sheriff; F. H. Jones, deputy sheriff; Stephen B. Corboy, court stenographer; Allen W. Reynolds, treasurer; Albert E. Starr, deputy treasurer; Thomas H. Patrick, recorder; Henry Rankin, surveyor; Andrew J. Zorn, assessor; A. C. Coates, coroner; Hannibal H. Loring, superintendent of schools.

COMMISSIONERS.—James E. Carson, president; James S. Fulton and Jacob Link.

IMMANUEL GERMAN LUTHERAN CHURCH.

Southeast corner Washington and Institute Streets. Rev. H. J B. Lange, pastor. Parsonage, 66 North Washington St. Services usual time. *Trustees*—C. Specht, C. Dreesen and C. Marquardt. *Treasurer*—H. Leetz.

LADIES' SOCIETY.—Mrs. C. Schwarzkopf, president.

GERMAN-ENGLISH LUTHERAN PAROCHIAL SCHOOL.—Corner Academy and Chestnut Streets.

PRESBYTERIAN CHURCH.

Corner Franklin and Jefferson Street. Rev. J. B. Fleming, pastor. Parsonage, 78 North Lafayette St. *Elders*—M. B. Crosby, A. V. Bartholomew, J. C. Pierce, D. C. Herr and S. L. Finney. *Trustees*—James McFetrich, A. L. Agnew, C. W. Dickover and George Finney. *Treasurer*—M. A. Salisbury. *Services*—Preaching Sunday at 10:30 a. m. and 7:30 p. m.; communion, first Sabbaths of January, April, July and October. Sabbath School, 2 p. m., A. D. Bartholomew, superintendent; S. Ross Martin, assistant superintendent; Miss Grace Jones, secretary.

LADIES' CHURCH ALLIANCE.—Mrs. D. M. Simons, president; Mrs. W. H. Gardner, recording secretary; Miss Margaret Beer, treasurer; Mrs. G. W. Windle, Mrs. M. A. Salisbury and Mrs. A. D. Bartholomew, executive committee.

Y. P. S. C. E.—Mabel H. Benney, president; Margaret C. Beer, vice-president; Chas. McDonald, treasurer; May M. Stickney, secretary. Meets Sunday evenings.

UNITY CHURCH.—LIBERAL.

Organized 1890. Rev. T. G. Milsted, pastor. Services every alternate Sunday at the Opera House. *Officers*—Hon. T. G. Lytle, president; Grant Mitchner, secretary; Wallace L. Wright, treasurer. *Trustees*—A. W. Vincent, H. N. Carver and Milan Cornell.

SOUTH VALPARAISO M. E. CHURCH.

Rev. John J. Thompson, pastor. Residence, 81 E. Main St., Valparaiso.

SALEM CHARGE.—Preaching every alternate Sunday at 10:30 a. m. and 7:30 p. m. *Trustees*—Thatcher D. White, Francis White, Daniel Stoner and Jacob Hall.

PLEASANT VIEW CHARGE.—Preaching every alternate Sunday at 10:30 and 7:30 p. m. *Trustees*—William Brown, Thomas Wilson and ———.

ST. PAUL'S (R. C.) CHURCH.

Northwest cor. Campbell and Chicago Sts. Very Rev. John Dempsey, dean.

ST. PAUL'S ACADEMY.—This Academy is adjoining St. Paul's Church, being in charge of six Sisters of Providence, where young ladies can receive instructions in all branches of music and the sciences, conducted on principles of home education. Address Sister Superioress (Sisters of Providence), Valparaiso, Indiana.

LIVING ROSARY SOCIETY.—This society numbers about 120 members, holds its meetings the third Sunday in each month in St Paul's Church, their chief objects being prayers, meditations and other exercises conducive to the salvation of souls.

SOCIETY OF THE CHILDREN OF MARY.—This society numbers about 40 members, meets in St. Paul's Church the second Sunday in every month for religious exercises, etc.

BOYS' SOCIETY.—Having a membership of about 40. Meets for religious exercises, etc., the first Sunday in each month in St. Paul's Church.

SOCIETIES.

ODD FELLOWS.

CHEQUENK LODGE, No. 56, I. O. O. F.—Jos. Holliday, P. G.; M. C. Skinner, N. G.; V. H. Wendt, V. G.; P. A. Marquardt, secretary; Frank Turner, treasurer; H. Stratton, W.; F. A. LaPell, Con.; J. J. Ferris, R. S. N. G.; Scott Norville, L. S. N. G.; L. A. Windle, R. S. V. G.; A. E. Starr, L. S. V. G.; John Ritz, J. F. Tolcott, S. S.; E. W. Hess, I. G.; J. E. Baum, John Sieb, J. W. Hagin, trustees. Meets every Monday evening at 7:30, at I. O. O. F. Hall, South Franklin Street.

FORESTERS.

COURT VALPARAISO No. 210, I. O. F.—Membership 75. Leonard Cline, chief ranger; Joseph Murphy, vice chief ranger; E. C. O'Neill, secretary; Frank H. Klein, financial secretary. Meets first and third Wednesday of each month at 8 p. m., in Horn's Hall.

GRAND ARMY OF THE REPUBLIC.

CHAPLAIN BROWN POST NO. 106, G. A. R., DEPARTMENT OF INDIANA.— Named after Chaplain Brown, of the 20th Indiana. Edward M. Burns, commander; John C. Flint, senior vice; Joseph Zea, junior vice; Aaron Parks, quartermaster; Dr. J. F. McCarthy, surgeon; John R. Mills, officer of day; John Ferguson, officer of guard; Robert Fryar, chaplain; J. W. Stratton, I. C. B. Suman and J. W. Elam, trustees; J. W. Stratton, M. L. DeMotte and Jap Finney, delegates to state encampment. Meets second Saturday and fourth Tuesday of each month at Old Masonic Hall.

MASONIC.

PORTER LODGE, No. 137, A. F. & A. M.—J. A. McConahy, W. M.; H. H. Loring, S. W.; F. Joel, J. W.; M. L. McClelland, treasurer; E. V. Arnold, secretary; W. T. Brown, S. D.; Wm. Lederer, J. D.; M. Winslow, J. S. Louderback, S. Meets first and third Tuesdays of each month, in Masonic Hall, cor Main and Washington Streets.

VALPARAISO CHAPTER, No. 79, R. A. M.—W. F. Mann, H. P.; Jonathan Osborn, K.; H. N. Renner, S.; H. H. Loring, C. H.; M. L. McClelland, treasurer; E. V. Arnold, secretary; J. D. Hollett, R. A. C.; H. Renfrok, 3 vail; J. W. Mocklee, 2 vail; I. Verden, 1 vail. Meets third Thursday of each month, in Masonic Hall.

VALPARAISO COMMANDERY, No. 28, K. T.—W. H. Gardner, E. C.; Jonathan Osborn, G. E.; E. D. Crumpacker, C. G.; H. N. Renner, S. W.; S. Ross Martin, J. W.; M. L. McClelland, treasurer; E. V. Arnold, recorder; W. C. Letherman, trustee. Regular conclave second Thursday of each month, at Masonic Hall.

KNIGHTS OF PYTHIAS.

VALPARAISO LODGE, No. 184, K. P.—J. H. Arnold, P. C.; W. B. Wasser, C. C.; J. A. Walker, V. C.; H. B. Darling, P.; Seth Eason, M. of E.; H. B. Darling, M. of F.; E. V. Willitts, M. of A.; E. E. Shedd, I. G.; A. B. D. Crow, O. G. Meets every Friday evening, in Hall, 13 W. Mechanic St.

ROYAL ARCANUM.

PORTER COUNCIL, No. 851, R. A.—J. M. Fabing, regent; C. S. Pierce, vice-regent; —— Watt, chaplain; Isaac Cornell, treasurer; C. W. Bartholomew, collector; M. Barry, auditor; L. M. Merton, warden; E. T. Chester, sentry; V. H. Wendt, trustee. Hon. M. L. DeMott, of this council, has been chosen as chief executive officer of the State. Meets every Thursday evening, in Royal Arcanum Hall, corner Main and Franklin Streets.

WOMAN'S RELIEF CORPS.

Mrs. J. W. Elam, president; Mrs. George Miller, senior-vice; Mrs. T. H. Pataick, junior-vice; Mrs. J. R. Drapier, treasurer; Mrs. A. L. Jones, chaplain; Mrs. Ed. Hunt, conductor; Mrs. D. Turner, guard.

OHIO CLUB.

O. P. Kinsey, president; A. L. Jones, vice-president; Grant Mitchner, secretary; H. N. Renner, treasurer; Cyrus Axe, J. H. Patrick and J. W. Stratton, executive committee; Mrs. C. J. Kern, Mrs. B. F. Perrine and Mrs. G. A. Dodge, ladies' auxiliary.

VALPARAISO BUILDING LOAN FUND AND SAVINGS ASSOCIATION.

A. P. Letherman, president; C. W. Dickover, vice-president; S. Ross Martin, secretary; John S. Louderback, treasurer; A. D. Bartholomew, attorney; A. J. Louderback, auditor. Meets last Saturday of every month, in Association Rooms, southwest corner of Court House.

EDUCATIONAL.

CITY BOARD OF EDUCATION.—H. M. Evans, president; James McFetrich, secretary; W. C. Letherman, treasurer. The public schools of Valparaiso are in a flourishing condition, having more than one thousand names enrolled. The board have just completed a new school building, which, for beauty and convenience, is unexcelled anywhere in this part of the country. An improvement much needed and highly ornamental to the city.

COUNTY BOARD OF EDUCATION.—Hannibal H. Loring, of Valparaiso, president; C. F. Leeka, of Hebron, secretary. Meets on the first days of May and September, each year, at the Superintendent's office. There are three high schools and one hundred district schools in the county, employing 113 teachers.

NORTHERN INDIANA NORMAL SCHOOL.—College Hill, south end College avenue. The largest normal school and business institute in the United States. Prof. H. B. Brown, principal; Prof. O. P. Kinsey, associate principal.

NORTHERN INDIANA LAW SCHOOL.—College avenue. H. B. Brown, president; Mark R. DeMott, A. L. Jones and H. A. Gillette, instructors.

Valparaiso City Directory.

Ablett, William, farmer; res 101 E. Mechanic.
Adams, Edward, res 27 So. Greenwich.
Adams Express Co., F. J. Ingram, agent, 10 E. Mechanic.
Adams, James, carpenter; res 9 W. Monroe.
Adams, Miss May C., dressmaker, 27 So. Greenwich.
Adams & Swartout, carpenter shop, 47 E. Main.
Agnew, Nathan L., Agnew & Kelly, 65 N. Michigan.
Agnew, W. W., 65 N. Michigan.
Agnew & Kelly, attorneys at law, 12 So. Washington.
Agart, John H., section hand, N. P.; res 13 South.
Albe, A., General Mdse., 6 W. Washington: res 13 Monroe.
Albe, Louis, clerk, res 13 Monroe.
Albe, Max, Gent's Furnishings; 8 Washington: res 39 E Monroe.
Albe, Samuel, clerk, G. Schwarzkopf, res 15 E. Monroe.
Albery, Harry B., prop. Valpo Steam Laundry, res 11 E. Institute
Alexander, John, carpenter. res 79 W. Chicago.
Allen, Charles T., jeweler (W. H. Vail), 7 E. Main; res 58 E. Jefferson.
Allen, Hale, students' supplies, res 67 S. College ave.
Allen, John R., watchman P. F. W. & C. Ry., res 55 W. Jefferson.
Allen, Mrs. H. R., dressmaker; res 55 W. Jefferson.
Ames, Fred E., brakeman, M. C. R. R,; res 52 N. Valparaiso.
Amos, Albert, hackman; res 14 E. Oak.
Anderson, Axel, laborer. res 43 N. Locust.
Anderson, Dr., E. F., physician: res 51 N. Washington.
Anderson, John, works clock factory; res 85 W. Main.
Andrews, L. Richard, carpenter; res 80 E. Jefferson.
Andreson, Chris., laborer; res West.
Angle, Solomon, Grocery & Confectionery, 64½ N. Morgan; res 64 N. Morgan.
Applegate, Ben. F., waiter, Grand Central Hotel.
Armentraut, Simon F., Mgr. College Hill Pharmacy, 59½ S. College ave.; res 5 South.
Arnold, E. V., undertaker and embalmer, 15 N. Franklin: res 68 N. Michigan.
Arnold, Ivan, farmer; res 82 E. Chicago.
Arvin, Fred. N., ins. agt.; res 63 E. Jefferson.
Arvin, John N., blacksmith, 45 E. Main; res 76 E. Jefferson.
Atkins, Dr. L., physician and surgeon; res 135 Locust.

Ault, John, fish peddler; res 99 E. Mechanic.
Ault, Willis; res cor. Broadway and S. Campbell.
Austin. Martin G., butcher; res 42 W. Jefferson.
Axe, C., Meat Market, N. Washington.
Axe, Cyrus; res 96 E. Jefferson.
Axe, Elias; res 36 N. Franklin.
Aylesworth, John W., Aylesworth & Dye, 21 Main; res 35 N Franklin.
Aylesworth & Dye, Boots & Shoes, 21 E. Main.
Bagley, Daniel, sr., laborer; res 25 Calumet ave.
Bagley, Daniel, jr., car repairer, C. & G. T. Ry; res 25 Calumet ave.
Baker, Harrison, well borer; res 29 E. Institute.
Baldwin, Miss Mandie E., teacher, N. I. Nrm.; res. 105 E. Main.
Baldwin, Wm., electric light trimmer; res 20 W. Water.
Ball, E., cashier, First Nat. Bank; res 37 N. Campbell.
Ball, Mrs. S. M., boarding; res S. Franklin.
Banister, Alfred, Ross & Banister; res 22 W. Jefferson.
Banta, Mrs. Alice, rooms, 1 Union.
Banta, W. H., Principal High School, 89 N. Washington.
Barber, J. W., mason-contractor; res 64 Freeman.
Barber, Wm. C., drayman; res 64 Freeman.
Barbour, Alpheus J., clerk, Lauderback's Grocery, res 17 So. Greenwich.
Barcome, Jos., laborer; res 21 Calumet ave.
Barcome, Miss Amelia, seamstress; res 21 Calumet ave.
Barcome, Victor, laborer; res 2 Dumas ave.
Barham, Geo. W., night clk P. F. W. & C. Ry.; res 65 E. Jefferson
Barnecko, C. F., blacksmith; res 54 E. Main.
Barnecko, Charles J., blacksmith, res 105 E. Mechanic.
Barnes, Mrs., Delina, boarding; res 73 S. Greenwich.
Barnes, James C., contractor; res 34 N. East.
Barnes, Jay E; res 85 E. Erie.
Barnes, Peter, janitor, Normal; res 84 College ave.
Barnes, Walter B., salesman, J. Lowenstine; res. 63 E. Erie.
Barnholt, Chris., Meat Market, Mechanic, res 9 Spring.
Barry, David, blacksmith, 37 W. Main; res. 26 W. Mechanic.
Barry, Michael, blacksmith & wagonmaker, 13—17 S. Lafayette; res 16 W Mechanic.
Bartels, John H., clerk, res 23 S Morgan.
Barthels, John, teamster, Blood & Lindner, res N E cor. Mechanic & Morgan.
Bartholomew, A. D., attorney, 6 Washington; res. 80 N Franklin.
Bartholomew, A. V., 80 N Washington.
Bartholomew, Chas. W., Finney & Bartholomew; res 96 N. Washington.
Bartholomew, Geo. F., cashier Farmers Nat. Bank; res 78' Washington.

Bartholomew, Girdon S., deputy county clerk, Court House; res Wood.
Bartholomew, S. L., insurance, Washington and Main; res 90 N Washington.
Bassett, George, teamster, 19 N College ave.
Bartlett, Miss Sadie, boarding, 71 S College ave.
Bastel, Eli, laborer, 2 Stokes.
Bastel, Samuel, laborer, cor. Stokes & Kinzie.
Bates, Demas D., law student, 45 N Locust.
Bauer, Fred'k. shoemaker, with M. La Force; res 20 E Mechanic.
Baum, Miss Eva, music teacher, 65 Union.
Baum's Hotel, J. E. Baum, prop., oppos. Grand Trunk Depot.
Baum, John E., prop. Baum's Hotel, res same.
Baum, Mrs. Hannah, rooms, 15 Freeman.
Baum, Niles L., rooms, 65 Union.
Baum, Wm., lather, 32 N College ave.
Beach, Geo. F., engraver & jeweler, 1 Main.; res North Franklin.
Beach, Mrs. Margaret M., rooms, 95 E Monroe.
Beach, Murray J., windmills, 46 N Morgan.
Bear, Mrs. L., 39 W Erie.
Beemer, John W., teaming, 106 N Washington.
Beemer, Mrs. Rachel, widow, 45 N Locust.
Beemer, Thos. R., farmer, 106 N Washington.
Beemer, Thos. T., 106 N Washington.
Beer, Dr. H. M., physician, 48 N Lafayette, res 14 W Chicago.
Bell, Erasmus, cashier First Nat Bank, res. 37 N Campbell.
Bell, Ernest A., planing mill; 75 E Main; res. 4 N Morgan.
Bell, Herbert R., drug clerk, E Jefferson.
Bell, Reason, liveryman, 58 E Mechanic; res. 61 E Jefferson.
Bender, Nick, 50 West.
Benham, Frost L., 90 E Jefferson.
Bennett, Geo. C., carpenter, 13 S East.
Bennett, Mrs. Kate, 2 Pearl.
Bennett, Miss Maggie, 2 Pearl.
Bennett, Mrs. Margaret, laundress, 37 E Institute.
Benny, Goldsborough C., gen. del. clerk Post office, 21 E Institute.
Benny, Mrs., 61 N Morgan.
Benny, Mrs. M. C., 21 E Institute.
Benny, Miss Mabel, teacher high school, 21 E Institute.
Bentley, Albert, carpenter, res 38 N College ave.
Bentley, Miss Frances, domestic, 51 N Napoleon.
Benton, Chas. W., teacher N. I. Normal, 105 E Main.
Beyer, Andrew, butcher, 49 W Mechanic.
Beyer, Fred., shoem., 16½ S Washington. res 49 Mechanic.
Beyer, Mrs. Philip, 49 W Mechanic.
Bidwell, 28 Union.
Biers, John, carpenter, Weston ave.
Billings, Geo. W., carpenter, 30 N College ave.

Billings, Scotter C., Columbia Bakery, 27 N Washington.
Billings, Terrence, stonecutter, 33 W Mechanic.
Binnamon, Henry, 33 W Mechanic.
Bissell, Joshua B., 45 E Monroe.
Bixby, J. D., night operator N. Y. C. & St. L. RR., 87 N Morgan.
Black, Miss Nellie, seamstress, 65 W Main.
Blades, Wm., 9 Cyrus.
Blair, Henry L., brakeman, P. F. W. & C. Ry., 6 Stokes.
Bleney, Wm., work train, C. & G. T. Ry., 54 N. Morgan.
Bliss, Chris., baker, 34 N Valparaiso.
Bliss, Reimel, 34 N Valparaiso.
Bloch, Mrs. Catherine, 34 Academy.
Bloch, John H., Stm Laundry, 40 W Main; res 34 Academy.
Bloch, Julius, Laundry, 34 Academy.
Bloch, Luther, 34 Academy.
Bloch, Martin, 34 Academy.
Blood, D. K., engineer, 33 E Monroe.
Blood, Fred., Blood & Lindner, Axe Ave & Limits.
Blood & Lindner, millers, 2 E Mechanic.
Bloomer, Frank, laborer, 7 West.
Bloomhuff, John W., carpenter, N College Ave & Erie.
Bloomhuff, Otis A., bridge carpenter, 97½ N. Lafayette.
Blunk, George, street sprinkler, 44 West.
Bogarte, M. E., prof. normal, 95 E Main.
Bondfield, 66 N Michigan.
Bondy, L., traveling salesman, 47 N Washington.
Bondy, L. D., Dry Goods, 5 E Main Grand Central Hotel.
Bonhold, Chris, Cornell & Bonhold, S Washington.
Bornhold, Claus, laborer, 17 South.
Bourke, Alphage, carpenter, 25 N Academy.
Bowman, Andrew J., teamster, 14 W Monroe.
Bowman, Chas., marble polisher, 34 S Lafayette.
Bowman, Emery A., plasterer, 43 N Franklin.
Bowman, Jos. E., paperhanger & painter, 43 N Franklin.
Bowman, Wm. O., iron molder, 43 N Franklin.
Bowser, Emerson C., barber, 81 E Jefferson.
Boyd, Mrs. Martha G., 68 E Chicago.
Boye, Hans, Saloon, 10 S Washington; res 52 N Franklin.
Boye, Miss Laura, 52 N Franklin.
Bozarth, N. J., Atty-at-Law, 18 S Washington; res 59 N Wash.
Bozarth, Mrs. Mary, 73 N Franklin.
Bradley, Guy, pressman, B. F. Perrine & Co.; res 107 E Main.
Bradley, John B., engineer, 107 E Main.
Bradley, Joseph, 23 E Institute.
Bradley, Mrs. Mary E., 51 E Monroe.
Brannard, Mrs. Bridget, 6 S Campbell.
Brazier, Henry, laborer, 68 W Jefferson.
Breiholz, Miss Lena, Cook Franklin House, res 10 West.

Breiholz, Max, laborer, P. F. W. & C. Ry., res 10 West.
Breitzke, Ida, domestic, 62 N Washington.
Brennan, John, teamster, 16 S Washington.
Brewer, Cassius, drayman, 20 N Morgan.
Brewer, Edwin B., printer, 40 S Lafayette Ave.
Brewer, John H., laborer, 60 N Franklin.
Brewer, Mrs. John H., Dressmaking, 60 N Franklin.
Brewer, Mrs. Lucinda, 40 S Lafayette.
Brewer, Matthias, 32 N Lafayette.
Brewer, U. S., printer & engraver, 40 S. Lafayette.
Brewer, Winfield E., painter, 40 Lafayette.
Brey, John, section hand, 4 Dumas Ave.
Breyfogel, Benj. F., teamster, 22 College Ave.
Breyfogel, Francis M., drayman, 12 S Napoleon.
Briscoe, Chas. F., 122 S Greenwich.
Brodie, John, Grain Merchant, 55 E Jefferson.
Brodie, Miss Theresia, domestic, 63 N Lafayette.
Brown & Co., Photographers, 20 S Locust.
Brown, Edward, jr., painter, 79 E Mechanic.
Brown, Edward, sr., 88½ E Main.
Brown, Edward L., painter, 88½ E Main.
Brown, H. A. W., Brown & Co., 20 S Locust.
Brown, Prof. H. B., Principal Normal, 53 E. Jefferson.
Brown, John, barber, 50 N Franklin.
Brown, Mrs. Jane, 50 N Franklin.
Brown, Miss Lucy A., Rooms, 3 & 5 Cyrus.
Brown, Mrs. M. E., 27 E Jefferson.
Brown, Myron, laborer, 14 South.
Brown, Sandy, 44 Locust.
Brownbridge, James, 61 N Valparaiso.
Bronson, P., Boarding House, 35 W Main.
Bruhn, Anna E., dressmaker, 83 Greenwich.
Bruhn, Claus, Cigars & Confy, 19 Union cor Locust; res same.
Bruhn, John, barber, 19 Union.
Bruhn, John, painter, 83 Greenwich.
Bruhn, Minnie W., dressmaker, 83 Greenwich.
Bruns, Wm. H., tailor, 75 E Monroe; res 41 S Morgan.
Brunson, Andrew, 22 E Institute.
Brunson, Oliver, 22 E Institute.
Brunson, Wesley, 22 E Institute.
Bryan, Miss Alice, laundress, 27 W Jefferson.
Bryant, Mrs. Alla, Drugs, cor Main & Washington, 90 N Wash.
Bryarly, Delbert, 115 E Main.
Bryarly, H. Paxton, 115 E. Main.
Buck, Theo., butcher, Cornell & Bonhold, 58 S. Franklin.
Buckley, Daniel J., wagonmaker, 8 N Weston Ave.
BUDD, CHAS. C.; jeweler, 6 Academy.
Budd, Rose, millinery with Mrs. Foster, 6 N. Academy.

Buel, Champ E., fireman. C. & G. T. Ry., 78 N Franklin.
Buel, Mrs. Eliza, 10 E Chicago.
Buel, Miss Ruth, Boarding, 33 W Mechanic.
Bundy, Frank, 136 E. Main.
Bundy, George, carpenter, 80 E Erie.
Bundy, Jay, works Ryans livery, 102 E Main.
Bundy, John R., section hand, 44 E Institute.
Bundy, Wm., carpenter, 56 W East.
Bundy, Mrs. Dora, Dressmaking, 44 Institute.
Bundy, Mrs. Wm., teacher, 56 N East.
Bunting, Harry, Pearce & Bunting, 14 S Washington.
Burgner, Mrs. Sarah, 79 E Main.
Burke, James, drayman, 69 N Michigan.
Burkhart, Martin, Farming, 14 Eass.
Burns, Edward M., township trustee, 73 E Chicago.
Burns, Mrs. Hanora, 18 W Monroe.
Burns, Miss Katie, waitress, 18 W Monroe.
Bush, P., works clock factory, 8 W Institute.
Bussard, Frank J., chief clerk Fort Wayne Depot, 62 W Main.
Cameron, A. B., portraits, res 18 W Jefferson.
Cameron, John W., Wilson & Cameron, res 66 N Morgan.
Campbell, T. Addison, flour & feed Mich City, res 42 E Erie.
Cape, James, nurseryman, res 7 E Union.
Capers, Isaac, res 38 N Morgan.
Card, Geo. F., shoemaker, res 29 S East.
Card, Frank, res 67 S Morgan.
Carleton, Hoyt, clerk, res 22 W Main.
Carpenter, John M., res 55 S College.
Carpenter, Mrs. Leah, boarding, res 55 S College ave.
Carr, A. O., grocer, cor Main & Lafayette, res 17 N Lafayette.
Carr, Benajah, hack line, res 33 N Lafayette.
Carruth, Alex., blacksmith, res 68 N East.
Carruth, Walter J., locomotive fireman, res 68 N East.
CARSON, Dr. J. C., Phy'n, res cor Monroe and Franklin.
Carter, —, 14 Walnut.
Carter, Geo., 1 Wayne.
Carters' Livery, 39 W Main.
Carter, Schuyler C., hack driver, res 35 W Jefferson.
Carver, Harrison N., teacher, res 15 S College ave.
Casbom, Lawrence, 21 N Academy.
Casbom, Sylvester V., 21 N Academy.
Cass, John E., lawyer, res 56 S Locust.
Cass & Weir, lawyers, 11 N Washington.
Castle, H. M., 45 E Monroe.
Castleman, Mrs. Catherine, boarding, res 21 Valparaiso.
Caswell, Henry C., Foreman Messenger office, res 22 N Fr'klin.
Central Card & Supply Co., m'f'g stationers, printers and engravers, cor Main and Washington,

Charbouneou, Miss Valeury, seamstress, res 94 E Main.
Chartier, Geo., locomotive fireman, res 9 South.
Chartier, Jacob, brickmaker, res 9 South.
Chartier, John, carpenter, res 4 Courtney.
Chartier, John, laborer, res 14 Brick.
Chartier, Marchal, barber, res 14 Wall.
Cherry, Calvin H., section hand, res 44 N Academy.
Chester, E. Taylor, drayman, res 23 S Valparaiso.
Chester, Sylvester, bartender, 21 S Valparaiso.
C. & G. T. R'y. depot Calumet ave, James McCree, agent.
Chicago Suit & Pants Co., R. P. Wolfe, agent, 10 E Mechanic.
Choate, Miss S. J. C., rooms, res 58 N Franklin.
Christian Tabernacle, Academy of Music.
Christie, Henry, carpenter, res 104 N. Lafayette.
Christie, Joseph F., laborer, res 104 N Lafayette.
Christie, Stewart, works Dulaney cl'k fac'ry, res 8 W Institute.
Christy, Arthur B., pos'l cl'k, P F W & C Ry, res 29 S Mich.
Christy, Wm R., cig's and conf't'ny, N E cor Mich. & Monroe.
Claussen, Claus J., tailor, res 21 S Locust.
Claussen, Hermann, tinner, res 21 S Locust.
Claussen, Jacob, sample room, 22 S Washington.
Claussen, John, janitor Pres. church, res 76 N Napoleon.
Claussen, Miss Minnie M., tailoress, res 21 S Locust.
Clay, John S., chief fr't cl'k Blue Island depot C & G T Ry, res Baum's hotel.
Clevenger, Miss Lola, b'kke'p'r Windles groc'y, res 105 N Wash.
Clevenger, Sylvester A., Covert and Clevenger, res 105 N Wash.
Clifford, Jeremiah, section boss C & G T Ry, res 83 N Napol'n.
Clifford, John B., railroad contractor, res 64 W Chicago.
Clifford, Patrick, res cor N Campbell & Haas.
Coash, Campbell, miller, Crosby & Son, res S Washington.
Coash, Lawrence, jr, bartender, res 39 Calumet ave.
Coash, Modest, milk dealer, res S S Nickel Plate ave.
Coash, Pelo, bartender, res S Franklin.
Coates, Hayes C., M. D., physician and surgeon, Washington st, res 16 S Napoleon.
Cobb, Mrs. Addie A., res 50 E Erie.
Coddington, Elmer E., portraits, res 110 E Jefferson.
Colborn, Abram, H. C. Johnson & Co., res Michigan City.
Cole, Martin B., 1 Wayne.
Cole, Mrs., 25 W Erie.
Coles, Miss Anna, teacher, res 88 N Franklin.
Coles, Friend W., commercial traveler, 88 N Franklin.
Coleman, James E., turner, res 43 S Greenwich.
Coleman, Nich, carpenter, res 43 S Greenwich.
Coleman, Mrs. Nich, boarding, res 43 S Greenwich.
Collins, Lewis L., car rep'rer C & G T Ry, res 23 Calumet ave.
Comford, Miss K., 113 E Monroe.

Commercial hall, college building, 60 College ave.
Conerty, Mrs Catherine, 9 Nickel Plate ave.
Conerty, Miss Rose, 9 Nickel Plate ave.
Consumers Commerc'l Co, John Fitzwilliams, agt, 3 S Franklin.
Cook, Mrs Olive, 34 N Franklin.
Coovert, Jesse L., drain tile, 107 N Washington.
Coovert & Clevenger, drain tile, Washington & Lafayette.
Cordill, Wm E., 39 N Lafayette.
Cornell, Mrs, 70 N Michigan.
Cornell, Chas., mason helper, res 32 N Morgan.
Cornell, Geo., laborer, res 9 W Water.
Cornell, Isaac, grocer, E Main, res E Chicago cor Morgan.
Cornell, Milan, stock dealer, res 74 N Michigan.
Cornell, Ross K., Cornell & Bonhold, 61 E Chicago.
Cornell & Smith, grocery store, 19 E Main.
Cornell, William, laborer, 9 W Water.
Cornell & Bonhold, meat market, 8 E Mechanic.
Coudrey, Frank, eng. P F W & C Ry, res 9 S Weston ave.
Courtwright, Adrian, rooms, res 60 S Locust.
Courtwright, Samuel F., boarding, res 30 S Locust.
Courtwright, William D., boarding, res 61 S College ave.
Couture, Mrs Delda, rooms, res 18 College ave.
Cowley, Miss Abbie W., tc'h'r public sch'l, b'ds 22 College ave.
Coyer, Frank, laborer, 30 W Water.
Cram, Hiram, horse trainer, res 27 Billings.
Crisman, Charles, printer, Vidette, res 30 W Chicago
Crisman, Frank, printer, Vidette, res 30 W Chicago.
Crisman, Oliver, laborer, 30 W Chicago.
Crosby & Son, millers, 9 W Mechanic, mills, 72 Washington.
Crosby, Freeman, Crosby & Son, res 72 S Washington.
Crosby, M. B., Crosby & Son, res 72 S Washington.
Crosby, Ness, b'kk'per Crosby & Son, res 72 S Washington.
Cross, Nahum, carpenter, res 59 N Michigan.
Crouso, Geo. W., painter, res 111 N Washington.
Crow, Chas., carpenter, res 13 E Oak.
Crow, Mrs. Emma, carpet weaver, res 97 N Lafayette.
Crumpacker, E. D., judge appellate court, res 31 E Jefferson.
Crumpacker, Theo., 78 E Jefferson.
Culven, George W., 80 N Lafayette.
Culven, Mrs. Geo. W., medicines, res 80 N Lafayette.
Culver. Jos. M., plasterer, res 9 Stokes.
Cunningham, Elmer E., vet surg'n, 38 S Wash, res 42 S Wash.
Currier, John M., carpenter, 32 W Monroe.
Currier, N. P., farmer, res 64 E Erie.
Curtain, Thomas, section hand, res 106 W Main.
Curtis, C. W., 87 College ave.
Dade, Tiny, domestic, 78 N Lafayette.
Dahl, Nellie, 43 S East.

Dailey, Mrs. M. A., housekeeper, 61 N Napoleon.
Daily, Patrick, Daily & Reagan, N. Napoleon.
Daily & Reagan, saloon, 26 W Main.
Daily and Weekly Star, The, J. A. McConahy, publisher, 12 S. Washington.
Dale, Edw. L., stenographer, 9 E Oak.
Dale, John G., laborer, Calumet av. & Elm.
Dale, Miss Nora, dressmaking, 9 E Oak.
Dale, Wm. P., janitor, Christian Church, 9 E Oak.
Dalton, Mrs. Nora, 78 W Jefferson.
Dalton, Miss Ella, seamstress, 78 W Jefferson.
Dalton, Miss Lizzie, clerk, 78 W Jefferson.
Daly, Wm., 9 N Napoleon.
Daly, Mrs. Bridget, 9 N Napoleon.
Daly, Mrs. M., dressmaker, 57 W Jefferson.
DARLING, HARRY B., newspaper correspondent, 39 W. Erie.
Davis, Miss Inez, teacher, Public School, bds 21 E Water.
Davis, Perry, night baggageman C & G T Ry, 51 Calumet ave.
Davis, Reuben R., mill hand, 15 Western ave.
Davis, Wm., freight clerk, C & G T Ry, 51 Calumet ave.
Dawson, Nathan, windmills, Dolson & Cain, res 50 E Erie.
Dayton, Mrs. Fannie, teacher, 45 S East.
Dean, Elmira, Mrs., rooms, S College ave.
Dean, Lyman E., Valp. Plumbing Co., 30 N Lafayette.
Decker, Chas., bds 10 Lytle.
Decker, Joseph, agent for Chicago Supply Co., 17 W Main; res 61 W Main.
Decrow, John B., farmer, 67 E Jefferson.
Deming, Charles, painter, 40 N Academy.
Deming, O. H., carpenter, 40 N Academy.
Dempsey, Rev., Father, pastor St. Paul's Catholic Church, 56 W Chicago.
De Motte, Mark L., postmaster, 71 N Franklin.
De Motte, Wm. C., undertaker, with Finney & Bartholomew, 21 S Franklin.
Demming, Miss Lizzie, 25 W Erie.
De Patis, Paul, laborer, 59 Axe.
Deshler, Lewis, 71 E Chicago.
Dewells, Joseph, 27 N Academy.
De Witt, John W., coal dealer, 19 So Greenwich.
De Witt, R. C., 43 S East.
Dickinson, Mrs. Estella D., rooms, 19 East Water.
Dickover, Chas., W., contractor. 76 N Franklin.
Dickover, Chas. H., brickmason, 91 N Franklin.
Dickover, Mark L., assistant postmaster, 76 N Franklin.
Diefenbaugh, Miss Estella, teacher high school, 28 E Monroe.
Diefenbaugh, Mrs. Louisa, 28 E Monroe.

Diemoh, Levi, Sexton-Cemetery, 14 Weston ave.
Dille, Calvin L., farmer, 51 N Franklin.
Dille, E. W., carpenter, 67 E Main, res 71 E Main.
Dille, Stephen, Tobacco & Confectionery, 74 S Franklin.
Dillingham & Munger, Flour & Feed, 24 E Mechanic.
Dillingham, Stanton, Dillingham & Munger, res 102 E Main.
Dillingham, Mrs. Elma, boarders, 27 N. Washington.
Dillon, Mrs., cor Boundary & S Campbell.
Dodge, Geo. A., agent P H W & C Ry, 32 W Mechanic.
Dodge, Geo. M., operator, W U Telegraph, 48 W Mechanic.
Doege, August, 33 S Locust.
Dolson, Geo. H., horses & cattle com., 51 E Mechanic.
Dolson, Glen S., salesman, 85 E Main.
Dolson, Jesse, 109 E Main.
Dolson, S. W., Dolson & Talbert, 78 E Main.
Dolton, Lizzie, saleslady, 78 W Jefferson.
Dolson, Silas W., Dolson & Talbert, E Main, res 85 E Main.
Dolson & Talbert, grocery, 17 E Main.
Dornte, Wm. H., car inspector, P F W & C Ry, 46 N Campbell.
Dotzer, Hugh, pressman, B. F. Perrine & Co., 100 N Franklin.
Dougherty, O. M., Insurance, 6 S Washington, res 3 S Franklin.
Dowdell, Wm., H., lawyer, 1 S Franklin., res 103 E Mechanic.
Doyle, J. L., barber, under Bryants Drug St., res 72 N Lafayette.
Drago, Grant, conductor, P F W & C Ry, 45 W Chicago.
Drago & Sievers, Misses, Dressmaking, 15 N Washington.
Drago, Mrs. S. C., Dressmaking, 33 N Napoleon.
Drago, Wm. F., blacksmith with T. B. Louderback, 50 E Main.
Drake, Reuben, laborer, 104 W Main.
Drake, Wm. H., laborer, 104 W Main.
Drapier, Miss Grace, High school teacher, 7 E Chicago.
Drapier, Jas. R., Insurance, 7 E Chicago.
Drapier, Hal. D., clerk, 7 E Chicago.
Drapier, Myron J., salesman, 7 E Chicago.
Drawns, Frederick W., farmer, 23 S College Ave.
Dreesen, Claus, bricklayer, 27 S College Ave.
Drombold, Mrs. David, 7 W Kinzie.
Droom, Edgar E., traveling salesman, 103 N Washington.
Drowns, A. O., conductor, Fort Wayne RR, 30 W Jefferson.
Duclos, Joseph, 104 N. Lafayette.
Duerr, Fred'k. B., clerk, 65 E Wood.
Du Laney Clock Company, J. W. Du Laney, Supt., cor Campbell and Water.
Du Laney, C. F., wks clock factory, 6 Calumet Ave.
Du Laney, J. W., Supt. Du Laney Clock Co., 63 N Lafayette.
Dulch, Henry, mill hand, 79 W Chicago.
Dumas, Moses, 12 South.
Dunham, Chas. M., machinist, 57 S Washington.
Dunham, Obediah, 63 S Washington.

Dunlap, John C., contractor, 9 E Institute.
Dunlap, Miss May, Waitress, Grand Central Hotel.
Dunlap, R. A., clerk, 26 Campbell.
Dunning, John, 74 N Washington.
Du Patis, Hattie, domestic, 80 N Franklin.
Durand, David, laborer, 79 S Greenwich
Durand, George, laborer, 107 N Lafayette.
Durand, Gilbert, Last house N Washington.
Durand, Jos., brick maker, Last house N Washington.
Durand, Lucy, nurse, 62 E Main.
Duval, Mrs. Sylvester, seamstress, 12 E Mechanic.
Dye, H. W., Aylesworth & Dye, 60 S Franklin.
Dye, Mrs. Christina, 41 N Academy.
Dye, Mrs. Aurelia, seamstress, 37 N Academy.
Dye, Wm. H., carpenter, 32 N Locust.
Dygert, Horace, laborer, 10 Lytle cor Bush.
Earl, Edward H., ice merchant, res 30 N Morgan.
Eason, Miss Hattie, clerk, Bondy's store, boards 80 N Franklin.
Eason, Seth, clerk, res 82 N Franklin.
Easterday, Chas, laborer, 36 E Institute.
Easterday, John, brakeman P F W & C Ry, res 38 W Jefferson.
Ebersold, Fr'dr'k C., saloon keeper, Mich Cy, res 31 N Nap'ln.
Eddy, Glen G., tel'h operator C & G T Ry, res 92 N Franklin.
Edelman, John B., baker, res 38 W Mechanic.
Edwards, Wm L., mason, res 125 E Main.
Eglin, Frank, cor Wayne & W Chicago.
Eglin, John, milk, res cor Wayne & W Chicago.
Ehrhardt, Arthur, boarding house, res 59 S Greenwich.
Eifler, Geo William, teacher, res 33 S Locust.
Eikenberry, B. F., 129 S Locust.
Elam, John W., county auditor, court house, res 46 N Lafay'te.
Elam, Mrs J. W., dep auditor, court house, res 46 N Lafayette.
Elam, Miss Salina, dep auditor, c't house, res 46 N Lafayette.
Elam, Warren, works clock factory.
Ellis, William L., marble cutter, res 34 E Jefferson.
Ely, C. C., 131 S Greenwich.
Englehorn, Jacob, baker, Windle grocery, res N Franklin.
English, John J., railroad laborer, res 49 S Morgan.
Ennis, Geo., bartender, boards Grand Central hotel.
Erea, Joe, works clock factory.
Erie, Mrs Andrew, widow, 11 S Campbell.
Estell, Guy, engineer C & G T Ry, res 25 E Elm.
Evans, Guy H., clerk, Letherman's drug store, res 77 E Erie.
Evans, H. M., M D, 15 E Monroe, res 10 E Monroe.
Evans, Isaac W., teacher, res 77 E Erie.
Evans, Walter H., teacher, 77 E Erie.
Fabing, John M., operator, N Y C & St. L. R. R. res 11 South.
Falcom, — 83 E Main.

Faley, Frank, gents f'rn'hing goods, 9 E Main, res 86 E Wash.
Fanning, John, brakeman, res 28 Academy.
Fanning, Mrs Josie, foot of S Napoleon.
Faradise, Henry, carpenter, res 58 N Campbell.
Faradise, Thos., carpenter, res 58 N Campbell.
Faucher, August, rooms, 55 S College ave.
FAUNCE, JOHN, rustic chair maker, res 61 S Fr'klin.
Felton, John M., livery, res 50 E Mechanic.
Felton, Robert L., livery stable, 48 E Main, res 50 E Mechanic.
Ferguson, John, painter, res 2 Horse Prairie ave.
Fernandez, Frank, tobacco & confections, 23 S Franklin.
Fernekes, Chas., bakery & confectionery, 8 Main.
Fernekes, Chas H., clerk, 8 Main.
Fessender, Mrs May, rooms, res 74 E Mechanic.
Fickle, David B., Agnew & Kelly.
Field, George E., carpenter & Florist, res 11 LaPorte ave.
Fields, Ralph, carpenter, res 40 E Mechanic.
Findling, Fred W., clerk, res 5 Factory.
Findling, Henry M., tinner, res 93 N Franklin.
Finley, Miss J. E., night op'r, P F W & C Ry, res 18 N Laf't.
Finney, Miss Ella M., teacher, res 39 N Michigan.
Finney, Ernest, clerk, Specht & Finney, res 39 N Michigan.
Finney, Geo W., street commissioner, res 39 N Michigan.
Finney, Stephen L., Specht & Finney, E Main, res 37 E Ch'go.
Finney, Wm B., Finney & Bartholomew, res 13 N Morgan.
Finney & Bartholomew, furn're & undertaking, 21 S Franklin.
Fire engine house, 16 & 18 E Mechanic.
First Baptist ch'ch, cor Lafayette & Chicago, Dr Heagle, pastor.
First M E church, Rev Allen Lewis, pastor, n w cor Franklin & Jefferson.
First National Bank of Porter county, 12 S Washington.
First Presbyterian church, cor Jefferson & Franklin, Rev J. B. Fleming, pastor.
Fish, Geo H., boards Grand Central hotel.
Fish, Herbert J., farmer, res 101 E Main.
Fishburn, John, 39 E Erie.
Fishburn, Wm, 55 S Franklin.
Fisher, Theodore, salesman, res 121 E Main.
Fiske, Mrs. Sadie A., W Main.
Fitzwilliams, Miss Fannie I., b'kk'per, res 40 E Monroe.
Fitzwilliams, John, insurance agent, 40 E Monroe.
Flake, Geo., 56 W Main.
Flaugher, Albert, sawyer, res. 39 N College ave.
Flaugher, Jas. A., locomotive fireman, 39 College ave.
Flaugher, Miss Jennie, dressmaker, 39 N College ave.
Fleming, Ben., drayman, 63 E Main.
Fleming, Henry, well borer, 78 E Main.
Fleming, Rev. J. B., pastor Pres church, 78 N Lafayette.

Fleming, J. F., watchman Nickel Plate crossing, Nickel Plate ave.
Fleming, John S., Carpenter, res 3 S. Locust
Fleming, Lincoln, laborer, 8 Lytle.
Flewellen, Mrs. A., laundress, 32 Locust.
Flint, Austin V., boarding, 47 S College. ave.
Flint, John C., rooms, 22 Union.
Flynn, James, laborer, 24 W Water.
Forney, J. W., 65 Freeman.
Foster, Allen P., salesman, 8 S Washington.
Foster, Chas., bookkeeper, N E cor. Locust & Main.
Foster, Jeremiah, carpenter, 93 E Main.
Foster, John L., teamster, 36 W Chicago.
Foster, Louis, brickmaker, 66 Union.
FOSTER, MRS. N. B., Millinery, 8 S Washington.
Fox, John W., blacksmith, 64 N Campbell.
Fowler, Mrs. Hettie, domestic, 74 N Michigan.
Fox, Christian, laborer, 61 N Lafayette.
Fox, George, carpenter, 6 Pearl.
Fox, Jacob, carpenter, 64 N Campbell.
Fox, Martin, Section hand, 64 N Campbell.
Frakes, Daniel, house mover, cor Valparaiso & Institute.
Frakes, Miss Jennie, seamstress, 46 E Institute.
Frakes, Miss Maud M., compositor, 46 E Institute.
Frakes, Mrs. Sara, 46 E Institute.
Frame, Edward N., 76 N Michigan.
Franco, Artur, clerk, 31 N Academy.
Franklin Hotel, Paul Nupnau, prop., cor. Mechanic & Campbell.
Frazier, Mrs. C. A., rooms, 35 Union.
Frechett, John, shoem., with M. La Force, res 20 W Mechanic.
FREEMAN, WM. & CO., Merchants, 23 East Main; 58 N. Lafayette.
French, Sylvia, S East cor Water.
French, Mrs. S. L., 25 N East.
Fryar, Robert M., 107 E Monroe.
Fuller, Luther, 39 S Lafayette.
Fuller, Amasa, 75 E Chicago.
Fuller, Charles, 39 S Lafayette.
Galbreath, Edgar, clerk, 14 S Washington.
Gall, Chas., laborer, 26 W Water.
Gall, John, laborer, 26 W Water.
Galloway, Reader, carpenter, 57 W. Mechanic.
Gant, Miss Cydonie, rooms 57 Calumet Ave.
Gant, Miss Flora, Room 57 Calumet Ave.
Gardner, Eliza, laundress, 34 Freeman.
Gardner, E. J., bookkeeper, Farmers Natl. Bank, 81 N Morgan.
Gardner, Henry B., Boarding House, 34 Freeman.
Gardner, Joseph, Pres. Farmers Natl. Bank, 31 N Washington.
Gardner, Mrs. Christina, 21 N Valparaiso.

Gardner, W. H., V. P. Farmers Natl. Bank, 55 N Washington.
Gasser, Fred, 41 Napoleon.
Geiselman, Emery, student, 83 College Ave.
Geiselman, James, student, 83 College Ave.
Geiselman, Lillie M., Rooms, 83 College Ave.
German Lutheran Church, s. w. cor Washingt. & E Institute.
German Lutheran Immanuel School, 13 N Academy.
Gillett, H. A., lawyer, 1 S. Franklin, res 10 N College Ave.
Gilbert, Mrs. Lucinda, Boarding, 74 S Morgan.
Glass, Max, tailor, 46 Napoleon St.
Glover, Alfred, laborer, 46 N Locust.
Glover, Jos., carpenter, 44 Valparaiso St.
Glass, Max, tailor, 46 N Napoleon.
Gogan, Chas. M., engineer, Fort Wayne RR, 57 W Main.
Goodger, John, 28 E Oak.
Goodperlet, Miss Lena, domestic, 55 N Washington.
Goodwin, Anson H., 32 W Monroe.
Gould, Mrs. Lottie, Boarding, 23 N Lafayette.
Gower, Rev. E. L., 76 E Jefferson.
Gray, James J., mail carrier, 65 N Morgan.
Gray, William, brakeman, P F W & C Ry., 65 N Morgan St.
Gray, William T., General Store, 30 W Main, res 67 Union.
Green, Jay M., manager Specht & Finney, 59 College Ave, res 62 Union.
Green, Miss Lizzie, dressmaker, 93 N Napoleon.
Greenert, Chris., wks P Ft W & C Ry, 70 W Jefferson.
Greenert, Mrs. W., 70 W Jefferson.
Gregory, Edw. D., Police Dept., 60 N. Morgan.
Greyson, Agnes, waitress, 47 E Main.
Greyson, Chas., conductor, C & G T Ry, 33 Calumet Ave.
Greyson, Chas. K., Bakery, 61 N Napoleon.
Greyson, A. S., Bakery and Lunchroom, 47 E Main.
Gribbohm, Hans, laborer, 77 E Union.
Gribbohm, Peter, clerk, 77 Union.
Griebel, F. J., barber, 7 W Main.
Griffin, Ed. H., Telegr. operator, C & G T Ry, 92 N Franklin.
Griffin, Jos. A., mason, 29 N Greenwich.
Griffin, Oliver, teamster, 29 N Greenwich.
Griffith, Lewis, laborer, 10 Lytle.
Grimes, Mrs. Mary, 15 W Water.
Grimes, Wm., section hand, Ft W RR, 15 W Water.
Griswold, A. J., farmer, 106 N Franklin.
Griswold, Jesse L., farmer, 106 N Franklin.
Griswold, James, blacksmith, 34 E Mechanic.
Groff, J. H., Boarding House, 99 College Ave.
Groth, Miss Grace, music teacher, 23 S Greenwich.
Günther, August, carpet weaver, near Clock factory.
Gunther, Miss Paulina, domestic, 77 N Franklin.

Gardner, W. H., V. P. Farmers Natl. Bank, 55 N Washington.
Gasser, Fred, 41 Napoleon.
Geiselman, Emery, student, 83 College Ave.
Geiselman, James, student, 83 College Ave.
Geiselman, Lillie M., Rooms, 83 College Ave.
German Lutheran Church, s. w. cor Washingt. & E Institute.
German Lutheran Immanuel School, 13 N Academy.
Gillett, H. A., lawyer, 1 S. Franklin, res 10 N College Ave.
Gilbert, Mrs. Lucinda, Boarding, 74 S Morgan.
Glass, Max, tailor, 46 Napoleon St.
Glover, Alfred, laborer, 46 N Locust.
Glover, Jos., carpenter, 44 Valparaiso St.
Glass, Max, tailor, 46 N Napoleon.
Gogan, Chas. M., engineer, Fort Wayne RR, 57 W Main.
Goodger, John, 28 E Oak.
Goodperlet, Miss Lena, domestic, 55 N Washington.
Goodwin, Anson H., 32 W Monroe.
Gould, Mrs. Lottie, Boarding, 23 N Lafayette.
Gower, Rev. E. L., 76 E Jefferson.
Gray, James J., mail carrier, 65 N Morgan.
Gray, William, brakeman, P F W & C Ry., 65 N Morgan St.
Gray, William T., General Store, 30 W Main, res 67 Union.
Green, Jay M., manager Specht & Finney, 59 College Ave, res 62 Union.
Green, Miss Lizzie, dressmaker, 93 N Napoleon.
Greenert, Chris., wks P Ft W & C Ry, 70 W Jefferson.
Greenert, Mrs. W., 70 W Jefferson.
Gregory, Edw. D., Police Dept., 60 N. Morgan.
Greyson, Agnes, waitress, 47 E Main.
Greyson, Chas., conductor, C & G T Ry, 33 Calumet Ave.
Greyson, Chas. K., Bakery, 61 N Napoleon.
Greyson, A. S., Bakery and Lunchroom, 47 E Main.
Gribbohm, Hans, laborer, 77 E Union.
Gribbohm, Peter, clerk, 77 Union.
Griebel, F. J., barber, 7 W Main.
Griffin, Ed. H., Telegr. operator, C & G T Ry, 92 N Franklin.
Griffin, Jos. A., mason, 29 N Greenwich.
Griffin, Oliver, teamster, 29 N Greenwich.
Griffith, Lewis, laborer, 10 Lytle.
Grimes, Mrs. Mary, 15 W Water.
Grimes, Wm., section hand, Ft W RR, 15 W Water.
Griswold, A. J., farmer, 106 N Franklin.
Griswold, Jesse L., farmer, 106 N Franklin.
Griswold, James, blacksmith, 34 E Mechanic.
Groff, J. H., Boarding House, 99 College Ave.
Groth, Miss Grace, music teacher, 23 S Greenwich.
Günther, August, carpet weaver, near Clock factory.
Gunther, Miss Paulina, domestic, 77 N Franklin.

Gunther, Miss Nora, waitress, Grand Central Hotel.
Gunther, Miss Tillie, waitress, Grand Central Hotel.
Gustason, Aug., wks Clock factory.
Gutter, Geo., barber, 51 Monroe.
Haberle, Joseph, foreman coal chutes, res 9 Chestnut.
Haalck, Catherine, laundress, 9 Union.
Hall, G. A., 7 E Main.
Halladay, John G., carpenter, res 66 E Jefferson.
Halladay, Miss Mary, dressmaker, res 66 E Jefferson.
Halladay, Jos. W., carpenter, res 59 E Chicago.
Halmick, Mrs. Alta, domestic, res 80 N Lafayette.
Halstine, F. W., tailor, 11 E Main.
Hammond, Miss M. A., milliner, 3 E Main.
Hank, Chris, barber, res 86 N Napoleon.
Hanner, Milan, laborer, C & G T Ry, res 4 Lytle.
Hanner, Peter, 47 N Locust.
Hannon, Matthew, 45 Calumet ave.
Hanson, H. P., sewing machine agent, 42 W Main.
Hansen, Theo, barkeeper, res 31 Calumet ave.
Hansen, Thomas, laborer, res cor Boundary & Campbell.
Harbeck, John H., Harbeck & Rogers, S Laf't, res 116 N F'kl'n.
Harbeck, Miss Louise, domestic, boards cor E Chi'go & F'kl'n.
Harbeck, Wm. engineer, Blood & Lindner, 40 S Morgan.
Harbeck & Rogers, church furniture, 22 S Lafayette.
Hardesty, Mrs. Catherine, 83 E Monroe.
Hardesty, Schuyler C., br'k'n C & G T Ry, res 19 Calumet ave.
Harkless, Jos M., photographer, 41 S Union.
Harmon, E. P., 9 Cemetery ave.
Harms, John, works P F W & C Ry, res 9 Factory.
Harper, Miss Jennie, chair trimmer, res 35 N Washington.
Harrington, Elliott, drayman, res 12 Short.
Harris, —, brakeman, res 25 E Chicago.
Harris, Mrs. Jane, 81 E Monroe.
Harrold, Miss Bertha, 10 W Chicago.
Harrold, Harry W., 10 W Chicago.
Harrold, Miss Kitty, teacher of piano, res 10 W Chicago.
Harsh, Henry, 40 West.
Hart, Frank B., carpenter, res 46 S Locust.
Hart, Miss May, boarding, res 46 S Locust.
Hartnett, Maurice, w'chman, N Y C & St L R R res cor Spring & South.
Haskell, Miss Nancy, domestic, res 41 W Erie.
Haste, George S., Haste & Minor, res 56 N Mich.
Haste & Minor, hardware, 15 E Main
Hatton, Lewis, Hatton & Baylor, res 79 E Main.
HAWKINS, JNO. B., Justice of the Peace, 3 S Franklin, res 73 W Main.
Hayes, Sherman, laborer, res 7 West.

Haynes, Jos., painter, 17 S Greenwich.
Hayworth, Wm R., Furrier, res 65 N Lafayette.
Heagle, Rev D., D D, pastor 1st Baptst church, res 24 W C'go.
Heard, Thomas H., lawyer, 1 S Franklin, res 9 N Locust.
Heim, Clem, barber, res 46 N Napoleon.
Heinemann, Albert F., Heinemann & White, res 27 N College ave.
Heinemann & White, druggists, 59½ S College ave.
Hemell, Mrs B. E., 3 E Jefferson.
Henderlong Bros & Kirk, planing mill, 83 W Chicago.
Henderlong, Frank, Henderlong Bros & Kirk, res 11 Weston ave.
Henderlong Jos., mechanic, res 79 W Chicago.
Henderlong, Michael, Henderlong Bros & Kirk, res 79 W Ch'go.
Henry, William, agricultural implments, res 46 E Mechanic.
Henry, W. J. & Co., farming implements, 45 E Main.
Heritage, R. A., musical director, 109 College ave, Ind. state normal, res 16 College ave.
Herr, D. C., 61 N Morgan.
Herr, David H., 33 E Erie.
Herr, Frank, lather, 63 N Washington.
Herr, Miss Grace, clerk, 27 N Washington.
Herr, John S., 33 E Erie.
Herr, Mrs Phoebe, 33 E Erie.
Herrick, Cortes M., carpenter, 98 N Washington.
Herrick, Sheldon P., carpenter, 77 W Main.
Hess, Enoch W., Hess & Hoyt, res 16 N Lafayette.
Hess & Hoyt, restaurant, W Main
Hesser, Jacob, carpenter, 18 S Locust.
Hiatt, Miss Stella, retoucher, 40 E Mechanic.
Hibbard, H., teacher, 11 S College.
Hicks, Emma, saleslady, 23 E Main.
Hicks, May, 10 W Chicago.
Hicks, Wm. A., teacher, 48 E Monroe.
Hilficher, W. M., tinner, Ross Banister, 1 S East.
Hill, Leonard, farmer, 42 S Locust.
Hill, Leonard, jr., carpenter, 110 E Mechanic.
Hill, Peter, teaming, 46 N Franklin.
Hill, Wm., boarders, 34 Union.
Hilton, Harry H., machinist, 66 W Chicago.

[signature] photographer, 22 W. Main; bds Grand Central Hotel.

Hinkle, John, laborer, 78 E Chicago.
Hinkle, Miss Nannie, compositor, Daily Star, 78 E Chicago.
Hiss, A Emil, teacher, Normal School, 63 N Morgan.
Hixon, Loren, farmer, 95 N Washington.
Hofferth, Miss Tillie, domestic, 53 E Jefferson.
Hollatz, West.

Hollett, Jas. D., farmer, 40 N Washington.
Hollis, Robert, 58 N Franklin.
Hollister, Mrs. Henrietta, 135 E Main.
Holm, Jeremiah, bridge carpenter, 74 N Michigan.
Holstein, Fritz, tailor, 44 W Monroe.
Hootman, Rev. A. M., asst. past. Christ. church, 75 N Morgan.
Horine, Mrs. E. W., 67 E Erie.
Horne Bros., meat market, 12 Monroe.
Horne, Chas., farmer, 18 E Monroe.
Horne, Conrad, 18 E Monroe.
Horne, Jacob E., clerk, 18 E Monroe.
Horne, Lewis, meat market, W Main; res 22 E Monroe.
Horne, Peter J., stock dealer, 14 Main.
Horner, John H., 27 N Greenwich.
HORNFELD, A. J., dentist, 7 E Main, res N. Washington.
Horrocks, Martin V., carpenter, 20 E Oak.
Horrocks, William, Wm. Horrocks & Co., 20 Oak.
Horrocks, William & Co., printers and publishers, 20 Oak.
Howard, John, 7 N Academy.
Howard, John A., trainman, 40 W Jefferson.
Howe, John, saloon, 25 W Main.
Howe, Mrs. Thomas, 11 Wayne.
Howell, Wm. D., farmer, 73 N Franklin.
Hoyt, I. W., 9 W Monroe.
Hoyt, L. S., clerk, Grand Central Hotel.
Hughart, John W., janitor Court House, 26 W Jefferson.
Hughart, Mrs. H. D., 26 W Jefferson.
Humiston, George, traveling druggist, 63 N Franklin.
Hunt, Edward E., mason, 64 E Chicago.
Hunt, Miss Eva, domestic, 53 E Jefferson.
Hunt, Hubbard, retired merchant, 74 N Washington.
Hunt, Jas. W., laborer, 4 Lytle.
Huntington, James M., candymaker, 64 S Franklin.
HUNTINGTON WELLINGTON, Pianos, Organs and Sewing Machines, 6 W Jefferson.
Huntley, Alonzo, L., 81 N Morgan.
Hurlburt, Miss Jennie, 73 N Morgan.
Hurlburt, Myron, 73 N Morgan.
Hurley, Mrs. Celia, rooms, 91 S Locust.
Ingram, E. F., delivery clerk, Valpo l'ndry, res 96 E Mechanic.
Ingram, Frank J., agt Nat'l and Adams ex cos, res 53 S Fr'klin.
Ingram, Nelson D., 96 E Mechanic.
Ingram, Miss Rosa E, dressmaker, res 96 E Mechanic.
Irion, Miss Kate, assistant cook Grand Central hotel.
Irwin, Robert A., ext sw'h'n C & G T Ry, res 51 N Valparaiso.
Jackmore, A. J., laborer, res 7 Brick.
Jackmore, Geo., teamster, res 16 S Washington.

Jackmore, Jos., laborer, res 7 Brick.
Jackson, Mrs Matilda, 54 N Napoleon.
James, Edw L., carpenter, res 39 Valparaiso.
James, Mrs E. E., 50 N Napoleon.
Jaqua, Uriah D., 22 S Locust.
Jessen, Henry, laborer, res 6 Dumas ave.
Joel, Fred, dry goods & clothing, gents furnishings, 18 S Wash. res 62 N Lafayette.
Johann, John, laborer, res 70 E Erie.
Johnson, —, 124 S Greenwich.
Johnson, Miss Helen, waitress, Grand Central hotel.
Jones, Alonzo, drayman, res Oak, first house west of East.
Jones, A. Lytle, lawyer, res 8 Chestnut.
Jones, Ben F., works Felton's livery, res 48 E Main.
Jones, Bradford, 110 W Main.
Jones, Chas B., brakeman C & G T Ry, res 30 Calumet ave.
Jones, Clinton, stenographer, Agnew & Kelly, res 15 S Franklin.
Jones, David F., 31 N Washington.
Jones, Edwin, car insp'tr C & G T Ry, res 39 E Institute.
Jones, Frank P., mayor, city hall, res 8 Plum.
Jones, Frank, dep sheriff, res 8 N Morgan.
Jones, Grace G., teacher, res 8 Chestnut.
Jones, John L., stenographer, Cass & Wier, res 21 E Water.
Jones, Lemore, 60 N Lafayette.
Jones, Matt, manager Ryan's livery, res 15 S Franklin.
Jones, Miss, 10 W Main.
Jones, Robert P., real estate, res 22 N Lafayette.
Jones, Robert P., loans, 19 N Napoleon.
Jones, Roscoe C., Norris & Jones, res 7 Weston ave.
Jones, Telif, carpenter, 7 E Elm.
Jones, Tilman A., clerk, res 22 N Lafayette.
Johnson, Alb't A., salesman, res cor N East & E Elm.
Johnson, Andrew, laborer, 58 N Morgan.
Johnson, Miss Elma, waitress, Central hotel, res 58 N Morgan.
Johnson, Mrs. Gusta, carpet weaving, res 15 N Lafayette.
Johnson, Henry C., H. C. Jo'nson & Co, res N East & cor Elm.
JOHNSON H. C. & CO., lumber & coal, 64 N Valpara'o.
Johnson, J. E., works clock factory, res 40 E Jefferson.
Johnson, Mrs Lydia H., 76 E Jefferson.
Johnson, Ole, laborer, res West.
Johnston, Bryan, watchman P F W & C Ry, res 46 West.
Johnston, Wm., atty-at-law, 2 E Mechanic, res 73 N Wash'ton.
Jordan, Claus, 2 West.
Jordan, James, N Morgan.
Judd, Wm. A., station agent, Sedley, res 83 N Lafayette.
Jungjohan, Claus D., mason, res 20 West.
Jurdan, James, 75 Morgan.
Kamerer, Jacob, laborer, res 124 W Main.

Kane, Frank, farming implements, res 34 N Franklin.
Kane, Mrs. Rheuhamy, 34 N Franklin.
Katz, Samuel, tailor, boards Franklin house.
Keding, Ernest, carpenter, Ft W Ry, res 35 N East.
Keeler, —, locomotive fireman, res 90 W Main.
Keehn, Mrs. Callie, rooms, 32 S Locust.
Keene, Miss Ella, carpet weaver, res 97 N Lafayette.
Keith, Joe, works clock factory.
Kelley, George, eng, C & G T Ry, res 51 N Napoleon.
Kellogg, Alfred L., prop Kellogg mfg co, res 5 S East.
Kellogg, Mrs. Isador, 48 W Erie.
Kellogg Mfg Co, W Mechanic.
Kellogg, —, foundryman, res 49 N Napoleon.
Kelly, Daniel E., Agnew & Kelly, res Grand Central hotel.
Kelso, Sam'l, foreman r'ndh'se C & G T Ry, res 45 E Elm.
Keogh, Jas., clerk, res East Mechanic.
Kern C. J., genl mdse, res 57 N Lafayette.
Kerr, Miss Mary, domestic, boards 90 N Washington.
Kidd, Miss Emma, domestic, res 13 N Morgan.
Killinger, David E., works clock factory, res 8 W Institute.
Kimball, Harry, 26 E Erie.
Kimerer, Marion, lumber, res cor Elm and Valparaiso.
Kimer, Jasper, laborer, res 8 Spring.
King, Geo. C., locomotive fireman, res 24 N Valparaiso.
King, Wm. L., 25 W Mechanic.
Kinsey, Mrs. Elizabeth, rooms, 5 Brick.
Kinsey, Prof. O. P., asst principal N I N, res 86 E Monroe.
Kirchner, George, piano tuner, res 58 N Franklin.
Kirk, Lewis A., Henderlong Bros & Kirk, res 15 Weston.
Kirkpatrick, James, 31 E Elm.
Kirkpatrick, Mrs. Lizzie, 31 E Elm.
Kitchen, Geo. R., last house on E Oak.
Kitchell, Miss Ida, teacher, res 53 Franklin.
Kitchen, Harry W., last house on E Oak.
Kitchen, Rodney, teacher, res last house on E Oak.
Kitchen, Thos., Q., farmer, res last house on E Oak.
Knode, Scott, blacksmith, res 20 W Main.
Koch, John, Ft Wayne Ry, res cor Short and S East.
Kouns, Lafayette, painter, res 18 E Oak.
Krell, Mrs. J. D., 45 S Washington.
Kroll, August, laborer, res N W cor Oak and East.
Krull, Otto, cabinet maker, res 69 N Morgan.
Kruse, Peter, farmer, res 45 West.
Kuehl, Anton, clerk, G. Schwarzkopf, res 59 S Franklin.
Kuehl, John C., foreman Ft W Ry, res 59 S Franklin.
Kuehl, Lena, domestic, res 31 E Jefferson.
Kuehl, Mrs. C., 59 S Franklin.
Kuehl Sisters, dressmaking, 10 W Main.

Kull, Louis, butcher, res 5 S Franklin.
Kyes, Geo. W., painter, 56 Calumet ave.
Kyes, Harrison, laborer, res N Locust, N of C & G T Ry.
LaCount, Mary, cook Hess' restaurant, res 16 N Lafayette.
Ladauer, Lewis, painting, calcimining, res 27 S Morgan.
Ladauer, Miss May, 27 S Morgan.
LaDore, Dellie, waitress, res 47 E Main.
LaForce, Joseph, boots and shoes, 19 S Franklin.
LaForce, Mitchell, boots and shoes, 20 E Mechanic.
Lahan, —, laborer, res 143 E Main.
Lajess, Moses, laborer, P & Ft W Ry, res 54 N Campbell.
Lajess, Mrs. Mary, 54 N Campbell.
Lambert, Thomas, baker, res 2 Horse Prairie ave.
Landis, J. H., teacher, res 19 Mound.
Lancam, Lewis, 13 S College ave.
Lancam, Mrs. Mary, rooms, 13 S College ave.
Lange, Geo., laborer, res 32 West.
Lange, Jos., 32 West.
Lansing, Lee, works clock factory, res Boundary and S C'pbell.
Lansing, Lewis H., teaming, res cor Boundary and S Campbell.
LaPiere, Napoleon, painter, res 8 Dumas ave.
Latour, Henry, blacksmith, res 54 N Campbell.
Lattimore, Miss Mattie, rooms, 67 Union.
Laughlin, Mrs. J., 52 N Morgan.
Lawrence, Jacob A., traveler, res 13 N Napoleon.
Lawrence, Mrs. J., 65 W Jefferson.
Leaders, Carsten, 86 N Napoleon.
Leahy, Miss N. V., trimmer, 3 E Main.
Leahy, Wm., 16 S Campbell.
LeClair, Miss Annie, b'kk'per, res 5 W Chicago.
LeClaire, Chas., shoe maker, 9 E Main, res 93 E Mechanic.
LeClair, Harvey, clerk, Bondy dry goods, res 93 E Mechanic.
LeClair, Jos., LeClair & McNiese, res W Chicago.
LeClair, Mrs. Lenora, 15 Wayne.
LeClair & McNiece, groceries, 8 S Washington.
LeCount, Miss Mattie, 58 N Franklin.
Lederer, Wm. F., farm machinery, 31 W Main, res 13 E Ins.
Leetz, Henry, clerk, res 34 Michigan.
Leetz, Louis, clerk, res 34 Michigan.
Lehmann, Miss Annie, laundress, b'ds 106 N Washington.
Lemar, Joseph, laborer, res 78 S Franklin.
Lembke, Chas. F., architect and mason, res 28 N Morgan.
Lembke, Christian, bricklayer, res 81 N Napoleon.
Lembke, Chris. J., bricklayer, res 54 N Academy.
Lembke, Henry, mason contractor, res 14 Fass.
Lemster, Henry, contractor, res 87 E Mechanic.
Lemster, Thomas, mason, res 92 E Main.
Leonard, Alva, financial, 100 E Main.

Leonard, James, 16 W Jefferson.
Leonard, John, 25 N Napoleon.
Leonard, Mrs. Mary, 67 W Main.
Leonard, Patrick, laborer, res Broadway.
LEPELL, FRANK A., Undertaker, 11 W Mechanic.
LePell, Geo. W., eng'r electric light w'ks, res 15 W Mechanic.
LePell, John, furniture, 41 E Main.
LePell, Otto, painter and paper hanger, res W Main.
LePell, Wm., furniture, 32 E Main, res 84 N Washington.
Letherman, A. P., physician, 11 E Main, res 60 N Washington.
Letherman, Lawrence, P O inspector, b'ds 77 N Franklin.
Letherman, W. C., druggist, 1 E Main. res 67 N Washington.
Letter, Miss Mary A., dressmaking, res 87 E Main.
Letts, A. E., 9 W Erie.
Lewis, Rev. Allen, pastor 1st M E church, res 33 N Franklin.
Lewis, Oscar, barber, res 83 W Main.
Lewis, Richard, 57 N Valparaiso.
Lewis, Sylvester A., 106 E Main.
Libby, Mrs. Nathaniel, 16 W Monroe.
Lightcap Co., The, b'ksel'rs and sta'n'rs, res 105 College ave, cor Monroe.
Lightcap, W. J., Lightcap Co., the, res 103 College ave.
Lindgren, John, laborer C & G T Ry, res 23 Calumet ave.
Lindner, Chas. H., Blood & Lindner, millers, res 65 E Wood.
Lohse, —, traveling man, res 26 W Jefferson.
Lohse, Mrs. Able, 27 N Locust.
Lohse, Johanna, domestic, res 44 E Chicago.
Long, W. Mace, roadmaster P Ft W & C Ry, res 14 Wayne.
Longley, Edward, carpenter, res 7 N Campbell.
Longshore, Chas. W., carpenter and cont'r, res 56 N Morgan.
Longshore, Frank L., carpenter, res 45 E Institute.
Longshore, Geo., carpenter, res 43 Institute.
Longshore, Gordie, carpenter, res 43 Institute.
Loring, D. J., M D, physician, res 40 E Jefferson.
Louderbach. A. J., asst cash'r, F'st Nat'l Bank, res 85 N Laf't.
LOUDERBACK, J. S., Grocery and Bakery, 21 W Main, res 15 W Jefferson.
Louderback, T. B., wagonmaker and justice of the peace, 61 E Main, res 91 E Main.
Love, Jesse A., with Wm. E. Pinney, res 88 E Erie.
Love, Robert, farmer, res 88 E Erie.
Lowenstine, J., clothing house, res 62 N Washington.
Lowenstine, Maurice R., salesman, res 62 N Wash.
Lucas, J., works clock factory, res 8 Wayne.
Luddington, Alex, 42 Institute.
Luddington, Mrs. Elizabeth, 42 Institute.
Lutz, Chris, clerk, res 22 N Campbell.
Lutz, Ferdinand, clerk, 38 Main.

Lybarger, Chas., laborer, res 47 N Academy.
Lyons, Frank A., barber, 41 Union, b'ds 34 E Freeman.
Lytle, Don G., contractor and builder, res 32 N College ave.
McAlister, Jos. C., 20 College ave.
McAllilly, Jas. J., 98 E Jefferson.
McAlllilly, Miss Lizzie, teacher N Ind Nor'l school, res 98 E Jeff.
McAuley, Oliver P., prof normal, res 19 S Locust.
McAuliffe, Daniel, 74 W Jefferson.
McAuliffe, Florence, teacher, res 74 W Jefferson.
McAuliffe, Jerry, watchman, res 74 W Jefferson.
McAuliffe, John, messenger, res 74 W Jefferson.
McCallum, S. M., dry goods, 83 E Main, res 99 E Main.
McCALLUM, W. B., Dry Goods, 13 E Main, res 99 E Main.
McCarthy, John F., M D, physician, res 79 N Franklin.
McCarty, Mrs., Dennis, 6 Boundary.
McCarty, Jeremiah, brakeman P F W & C Ry, res 6 Broadway.
McClellan, H. M., restaurant, res 13 Mound.
McClellan, Mrs. Leah, restaurant, res 13 Mound.
McClelland, Marquis L., insurance, over Bryant's drug house, res 9 E Institute.
McClure, William H., jeweler, 21 E Main, res 68 E Erie.
McConahy, J. H., publisher daily and weekly Star, res 14 E Ins.
McCoy, George E., operator C & G T Ry, res 35 Calumet ave.
McCree, James, agent C & G T Ry, res 85 N Morgan.
McDaniels, A. W., day operator P F W & C Ry, res 18 N Laf't.
McDonald, Angus, car repairer C & G T Ry, res 43 N. Locust.
McDonald, Chas. A., bakery wagon, res 61 N Napolean.
McFetrich, Jas., White McF & Co., res 57 W Main.
McGee, Alex. J., carpenter, res 81 N Lafayette.
McGillicuddy Bros., Stewart marble works, 13 W Mechanic.
McGillicuddy, Jas., McG. Bros., res 47 S Michigan.
McGillicuddy, John, McG. Bros., res 64 N Michigan.
McGregor, John, locomotive engr, C & G T Ry, res 50 N Morg.
McGuire, Daniel J., asst. roadmaster, G T Ry, res 42 N East.
McIntyre, Samuel, boards 33 W Mechanic.
McIntyre, Samuel C., w'ks Dulany cl'k fact'y, res 32 E Monroe.
McKeehan, Chas. E., br'k'man, P & Ft W Ry, res 92 N Fr'kl'n.
McKeehan, David G., 81 N Washington.
McKenzie, Wm., hack and baggage line, res 75 E Mechanic.
McKeon, Peter, 100 W Main.
McLeaf, Mrs. D. A., boarders, 41 S East.
McLELLAN, JOHN W., Lumber and Coal, cor Washington & Monroe, res 57 E Jefferson.
McMullen, David, carpenter, res 61 S College ave.
McNay, James A., merchant, Freeman & Co., res 32 E Monroe.
McNay, Robert, teamster, 43 E Jefferson.
McNiece, Miles A., LeClaire & McNiece, res 93 N Napoleon.

JOHN W. McNAY,
MAKER OF
Artistic Wearing Apparel for Men

A COMPLETE LINE OF NOVELTIES IN ALL FABRICS ALWAYS ON HAND.

59 South Franklin Street, Cor. Monroe, Valparaiso, Ind.

McNay, John W., tailor, 59 S F'kln and Monroe, res 16 E W'tr.
McNiece, Nicholas R., grocery clerk, res 91 N Napoleon.
McQuade, Miss Florence, domestic, res 27 N Wash.
McSwords, —, Miller & McSwords, res 28 W Main.
Mahaffey, William, painter, res 88 E Main.
Magee, Daniel, w'hman, P Ft W & C Ry, res 43 N Academy.
Magee, John H., rooms, 36 W Mechanic.
Malcolm, Jasper, w'ks Valpo laundry, res 96 E Mechanic.
Maley, John W., shoemaker, care of Magee's, res W Mechanic.
Mandlin, Russell, 106 S Greenwich.
Mann, Albert, laborer, res S Mich and Ft W Ry.
Mann, Chas. F., gents fur'shings, 22 N Wash., res 63 N Wash.
Mann, David, 25 W Erie.
Mann, Henry, carpenter, res E Oak and limits.
Mann, Miss Stella, laundress, 4 S Campbell.
Mann, Wm. F., harn'sm'kr, 22 N Wash., res 63 N Wash.
Mandeville, L. H., 38 W Chicago.
Manville, Rev. Wm. S., 1 South, cor Franklin.
Marcy, Manley, harn'sm'kr, res 8 N Locust.
Marcellus, Wm. H., yd master G T Ry, res 39 S Wash.
Marine, Asa, 14 Billings.
Marine, Chas. H., real estate, S Franklin, res 40 N Morgan.
Marine, Lewis, S. S. Nickel Plate ave.
Mark, Joseph, second hand store, res 23 E Chicago.
Marks, Howard B., colonizing agt., res 68 N Lafayette.
Marquardt, Peter A., ins and real es'te, 5 W Main, res 72 E M'c.
Marquart, Claus, 91 E Monroe.
Marquart, Wm. D., mason, res 85 E Monroe.
Marshall, Frances E., farmer, res 75 E Erie.
Marshall, F. Ross, 75 E Erie.
Marshall, Ovington B., rooms, S. College ave.
Martin, Chas., cigar m'f'r, 24 W Main.
Martin, Christian, laborer, res 86 N Lafayette.
Martin, Hans, carpenter, 7 Factory.
Martin, S. Ross, city clerk, res 55 W Main.
Martins, Peter, truckman P Ft W & C Ry, res 19 W Water.

Norris & Jones, abstracts and real estate, 3 S Franklin.
Northam, Frank R., horse trainer, res 5 E Elm.
Nuppuau, Paul, prop Franklin hotel, cor Mech'ic and C'm'bell.
Nuppuau, Paul, sr, 11 Boundary
Nuppuau, Miss Rickey, dressmaking, res 11 Boundary.
O'Connor, Mrs. M , 57 W Jefferson.
O'Hara, Peter, engine wiper P H F W Ry, res 36 West.
O'Keefe, Mich'l, tob and confect'ny, 16 W Main res 30 N Nap'n.
O'Neill, E. C., county clerk, court house, res 70 N Lafayette.
O'Reilly, Michael, laborer, res 23 W Water.
O'Sullivan, Jas , laborer, res 35 W Academy.
O'Sullivan, Thos. J., boss section, P & Ft W, res 35 W Acad.
Oddfellows Hall, 9-11 S Franklin.
Oehlerking, Gustave, 5 Factory.
Ohlfest, John J., purchasing agt, res 55 S Michigan.
Osborne, Mrs. Mary E., 48 S Locust.
Osborne, William, drayman, res 102 E Mechanic.
Otis, Augusta, laundress, res 27 W Jefferson.
Overmeyer, Frank F., South.
P Ft W & C Ry, George A. Dodge, agt, depot foot of Main.
Pagels, Henry, tailor, 87 E Monroe.
Pagin, J. R., dentist, 7 E Main.
Pagle, Tillie, domestic, res 73 N Washington.
Paradise, Henry, carpenter, res — N Campbell.
Parks, Aaron, gunsmith, res 58 E Mechanic.
Parks, Mrs. C. E., 55 W Jefferson.
Parks, Frank B., lawyer, over Letherman's drug store, res 41 W Erie.
Parks, Samuel A., gunsmith, Washington, res 58 E Mechanic.
Parrish, Theodore, section hand C N Y & St L, res 15 Factory.
Patino, Louis, laborer, res 5 Weston av
Patrick, Miss Edith, deputy recorder, ct hse, res 17 N Locust.
Patrick, Jas. H., tinsmith, Main, res 57 N Michigan.
Patrick, T. H., County Rec., court house, cor Locust & Chicago.
Paul, Miss Deborah, dressmaker, res 18 W Jefferson ave.
Pearce, A. L., miller, 20 N Washington; res 21 N Napoleon.
Pearce, Benj. F., Pearce & Bunting, 14 So Washington.
Pearce, Mrs. George, res 43 N Napoleon.
Pearce, Geo. W., salesman, 14 S Washington; res 41 S East.
Pearce & Bunting, flour and feed, 14 S Washington.
Pearson, Olive, domestic, res 9 N Academy.
Peirce, Andrew J., traveling salesman, res 83 N Washington.
Peirce, Chas. S., boots & shoes, 7 E Main; res 51 N Washington.
Peirce, Jeremiah C., res 69 N Washington.
Peirce, Mrs. Joseph, res 4 Maple.
Peirce, Loring, clerk, res 4 Maple.
PENNOCK, B. F., harvesting machinery, 28 W Main; res 19 S East.

Pennock, Sam., student, res 151 S Greenwich.
PERRINE, B. F., bookseller and printer, cor College ave and Locust; res 125 S Locust.
Perrine, John B., stenographer, with Wm. Johnston; res 115 S College ave.
Perry, C. S., wks clock factory, res Grand Central Hotel.
Perry, Theo. H., brickmaker, res 7 Spring.
Peter, Miss Tillie, waitress, res 23 N Franklin.
Peters, res 114 N Franklin.
Peters, Chris., Peters Bros., 20 S Washington; res same.
Peters, Hans J., tailor, J. W. McNay, res 41 S Morgan.
Peters, Peter H., Peters Bros., 20 S Washington; res 44 E Chicago.
Peters Bros., saloon, 20 S Washington.
Petersvitch, Lawrence, section hand Ft Wayne R R., res 63 S Franklin.
Petit, Mrs. C. J., laundress, res 15 La Porte ave.
Petit, Harry E., tinner, res 15 La Porte ave.
Pettit, F. Henry, Windle & Pettit, res 41 N Michigan.
Philley, Hass, baker, works East Hall College Hill, res 112 N Franklin.
Philley, Wm. H., grocery clerk, res 112 N Franklin.
Picard, Prosper, carpenter, res 18 Academy.
Pickel, Michael, res 39 S College ave.
Pier, Perry, teamster, res 26 W Chicago.
Pierce, Andrew B., farmer, res 103 E Main.
Pierce, A. Warner, barkeeper, 10 S Wash'n; res 25 W Monroe.
Pierce, Chas. A., farmer, res 25 W Monroe.
Pierce, Leroy M., insurance agt. S Washington, res 97 E Main.
Pierce, Norman. B., farmer, 25 W Monroe.
Pierce, Simeon res 9 E Jefferson.
Pierce, Miss Tressie, domestic, res 25 W Monroe.
Pierce, Warner, farmer, res 25 W Monroe.
Pinter, Jacob, cigarmaker, res 5 N Campbell.
Pinney, Miss Loie, music teacher, res 49 N Lafayette.
Pinney, Wm. E., Pres. State Bank Valparaiso, 14 E Mechanic; res 14 E Mechanic.
Plahn, Detlef, milkman, res 18 West.
Pocock, Elias H., M. D., physician, res 2 W Institute.
Pomerenke, Henry, tailor, res 45 S Morgan.
Pomeroy, Geo., res 95 N Franklin.
Pomeroy, Loren, works Felton's livery, res 12 N Michigan
Poole, Miss Bertha A., clerk, 14 N Washington; res 63 S Michigan.
Poole, Mrs. Mary E., 63 S. Michigan.
Poppenhagen, John, laborer, res 30 West.
Porter County Jail, Sheriff, s e cor Mechanic and Franklin.
Powers, Thos., res 58 N Franklin.

Pratner, Walter Q., meat market, 15 N Washington; res 61 E Mechanic.
PRATT, THOMAS, Grocery, 38 S Locust; res 40 S Locust.
Price, Geo., res 16 N Washington.
Puntzky, Carl, shoemaker, Pierce; res 21 S Locust.
Purdy, Saml. D., barber, Washington; res 65 W Main.
Quin, Robt., res 69 E. Chicago.
Quinn, Wm. M., cooper, 57 S Lafayette, res 36 S Lafayette.
QUARTERMAS, GEORGE, Dry Goods, 4 W. Main and Water, res 21 E. Monroe.
Quinn, Wm., cooperage, res 36 Lafayette ave.
Racine, Timothy, laborer, 26 S Greenwich.
Raasch, Miss Augusta, domestic, bds 80 N Washington.
Rader, John H., general store, 83 E Erie; res 83 E Frie.
Radtke, Fred W., clerk, res 85 N Napoleon.
Radtke, Henry, laborer, res 85 N Napoleon.
Radtke, Tina, domestic, res 56 N Washington.
Radtke, Wm., laborer, 89 N Napoleon.
Ramsey, Sol, restaurant, Wash'n and Main; res 13 S Napoleon.
Randall, Mrs. Nettie, agent and canvasser, 44 E Monroe.
Raw, Edward, laborer, res 8 Factory.
Rawson, Geo., boarding house, res 27 Union.
Ray, James H., prop. "Hotel Ray," res 53 W Mechanic.
Ray, Wm. P., carpenter, res 91 E Erie.
Raymond, Louis, blacksmith, 44 E Main, res 7 Brick.
Reading, W. L., insurance agent, res 2 Calumet ave.
Reagan, Chas., Dailey & Reagan, res 39 N Mechanic.
Reason, Miss Emma, domestic, res 85 N Washington.
Redding, F. G, switchman, P. H. W. & C. Ry., res 62 W Main.
Reddington, John J., saloon keeper, 16 S Washington, res 17 W Monroe.
Redker, Adelbert, res 38 N College ave.
Reese, David, carriage painter, 13 S Lafayette, res 79 N Washington.
Rehder, Jerry, clerk, res 24 Academy.
Rehder, John, brick mason, res 24 Academy.
Rehder, Herman, laborer, res 5 Wayne.
Rehder, Marx, mason, res 24 Academy.
Rehder, Miss Anna, clerk, res 24 Academy.
Reifler, Andrew, carpenter, res West.
Renner, R. H., dentist, 9 E Main, res 48 N Washington.
Reynolds, A. W., county treasurer, court house, res 67 N Michigan.
Reynolds, William, clerk, res 78 E Erie.
Rhea, Mrs. A. H., res 79 N Washington.
Rice, Edwin W, res 89 N Franklin.
Rice, Nicholas, gardner, res W Oak 1st east of N East.

Rickard, Lewis A., purchasing agent, office with Heinemann & White, res 48 E Jefferson.
Ridgeway, Miss Anna, stenographer, res 80 N Lafayette.
Rigg, Sidney J., res 26 N East.
Riggs, William, res 21 S College ave.
Riley, Mary, waitress, Hess' restaurant, res 16 N Lafayette.
Ringleben, Adam, res N Locust, N of C. & G. T. Ry.
Ritz, John, res 11 Haas.
Roberts, Miss Essie, domestic, bds 4 Calumet ave.
Robinson, H. W., interior decorating, 12 Nickel Plate ave.
Robinson, James J., rooms, res 37-41 S Locust.
Robinson, Mrs. M. M., dressmaking, res 38 E Institute.
Rock, Judah C., clerk, res 11 N College ave.
Rockwell, Geo. S., purchasing agent, res 61 E Erie.
Rockwell, Wallace M., letter carrier, res 61 E Erie.
Roessler, John E., teacher, res 88 S College ave.
Roessler, Mrs. J. E., music teacher, res 88 S College ave.
Rogers, Mrs. J. B., res 31 W Jefferson.
Rogers, Roscoe, Harbeck & Rogers, res 31 W Jefferson.
Rohwer, Claus, laborer, res 47 W East.
Rose, Mrs., laundress, res 54 N Napolean.
Ross & Barrister, hardware, 38 W Main.
Ross, Richard D., Ross & Barrister, res 41 W Jefferson.
Rothermel, watchman, clock factory.
Rowe, Henry H., carpenter, res 26 N Morgan.
Rubin, Thomas, yard brakeman C. & G. T. Ry. res Oak.
Rudell, J., barber. 3 E Main.
Ruge, Claus, Ruge & Rathyen, res 84 E Main.
Ruge, Mrs. Emma, res 72 E Jefferson.
Ruge & Rathyen, saloon, 9 W Main.
Ruifrok, Prof. Henry, music teacher, res 104 E Main.
Ruifrok, Henry, Sr., res 104 E Main.
Rupke, John, section hand Ft. Wayne R. R., res 3 Union.
Russell, John, works clock factory, res 66 W Chicago.
Ryan, Dr. J. A. physician, 19 E Main, res 45 W Mechanic.
Ryan, James, section hand, P. & N. W., res 88 W Main.
RYAN'S LIVERY, Boarding and sales stables, res 13 S. Franklin.
Ryan, Michael J., brake'n, P. F. W. & C. Ry., res 28 W Water.
Ryan, Mrs. Mary, res 32 W Water.
St. Johns Church (German Evangelical), cor Water & Franklin, Rev. Henry Stabler, pastor.
Sager, Chauncey A.; res Axe & limits.
Salisbury, Jos. M., barber shop; 41 Union; res same.
Salisbury, M. A., stationery & music, 14 N. Washington; res 2 Haas.
Salvation Army Barracks, 27 W. Main.
Salyer, D. A.; res 40 W. Lafayette.

Sames, Landon P, painter, contractor: res 62 W. Mechanic.
Sames, Roy L., painter; res 47 N. Valparaiso.
Sampson, Wm., rooms 58 N. Franklin.
Sanborn. Mrs. Mary E.; res 2 Calumet ave.
Sargeant Bros., confectioners, 8 Washington.
Sauerberg, Chris., clerk, with Windle's grocery; res 129 E. Main.
Sauers, —; res 16 E. Oak.
Sayles, Marshall F., M. D., cor Main & Franklin; res 73 N. Franklin.
Sayles, Henry M., traveling salesman; res 84 N. Franklin.
Schellinger, Jesse B., laborer; res 102 N. Franklin.
Schneider, E., general store, 4 E. Mechanic; res 4 E. Mechanic.
Schneider, G. Henry, teamster; res 84 N. Lafayette.
Schneider, John, machinist; res 52 N. Napoleon.
Schneider, Wm., carpenter; res 49 N. Napoleon.
Schnewind, Henry; res 54 N. Lafayette.
Schuster, Joseph, laborer; res 25 Billings.
Schuld, Benj., dairy; res 24 N. East.
Schuld, Peter, dairy; res 24 N. East.
Schultz, John; res S. Franklin.
Schultz, Miss Pauline, domestic; res 96 N. Washington.
Schumacker, John, saloon, 9 S. Campbell.
Schuster, P. F., harnessmaker; res 3 N. Campbell.
Schroeder, James, saloon, 38 E. Main.
Schwarzkopf, Geo., grocer, 1 W. Mechanic; res 105 E. Mechanic.
Seebus, Claus C., laboring; res 52 West.
Sefton, Mrs. M. H., rooms; res 58 Locust.
Segerdahl, Wm., roadmaster C & G T Ry; res 26 Calnmet ave.
Sego, Annie, boarding; res 66 E. Water.
Sego, Ollie, boarding; res 66 E. Water.
Sego, Joseph, sheriff, Porter county jail; res cor Franklin & Mechanic.
Seirks, Miss Minnie, domestic; bds 89 N. Franklin.
Selman, Martin; res 48 E. Erie.
Shave, Mrs. Dora; res 12 West.
Shaw, George H., traveling salesman; res 9 Chestnut.
Shedd, E. seeds & plants, 31 E. Main.
Shedd E. E., nurseryman & florist, 35 Laporte ave; res same.
Sheets, August, teamster; res Laporte ave & city limits.
Sheets, Francis, teamster; res 82 N. Lafayette.
Sheffield, Burton, res Lafayette & Institute.
Sheffield, George, flour & feed, Hammond; res 10 Pearl.
Sheffield, Mrs. H., widow; res 65 N. Washington.
Sheffield, H., restaurant, Main & Washington; res cor Lafayette & Institute.
SHELDON, MISS GERTRUDE, Dressmaker; res 44 N. Napoleon.
Shepard, Miss J., res 149 S. Greenwich.

Sherman, Adam J., commercial traveler; res 4 Calumet ave.
Shinabarger, Edward, laborer; res 20 S. Campbell.
Shinabarger, Hugh P., carpenter; res 73 S. Locust.
Shinabarger, Jacob, teaming; res 3 Nickel Plate ave.
Shinabarger, L. D., oil & gasoline, cor Napoleon & Water; res 52 N. Valparaiso.
Shinabarger, Reason, gasoline and oils; res 15 W Monroe.
Shinabarger, R. Wesley, bridge carpenter; res 22 N. Lafayette.
Shinaman, Chas., conductor, P H W & C Ry; res 7 Wayne.
Shine, John; res 13 Wayne.
Shine, Mrs. Julia; res 13 Wayne.
Shoemacher, Miss Emma, kitchen girl; res 9 S. Campbell.
Shoemaker, Fred, bottler, 26 S. Napoleon; res 59 N. Napoleon.
Shoemaker, Mary, milliner, 4 E. Main; res 9 S. Campbell.
Sholl, Wm. H.; res 5 Haas.
Showalter, J. B., professor normal school; res cor East & Water.
Shreve, T. M., grocery, 10 W. Main; res 13 E. Water.
Shroyer, Oliver J.; res 115 Locust.
Shuey, Dr. F.; bds Grand Central Hotel.
Shuey, Mrs. D. F., cook; bds Grand Central Hotel.
Shuey, Geo. W., drayman; res 28 E. Elm.
Shultz, August, brakeman Ft. Wayne Ry; res 9 Kinzie.
Shultz, Otto, laborer, P & F W Ry; res 9 W. Kinzie.
Shultz, Wm., fireman, P & F W Ry; res 65 E. Chicago.
Shunk, Frank R., car inspector, P F & C Ry.
Sieb, J. W., meat market, 5 S. Franklin; res 69 E. Mechanic.
Siebert, Fritz, switchman; res 55 S. Morgan.
Sievers, Egert, clerk; res 60 E. Erie.
Sievers, John, druggist, 1 E. Main; res 40 E. Main.
Sievers, Jacob H., saloon, 40 E. Main.
Sievers, Hans, saloon, 41½ Calumet ave; res 41 Calumet ave.
Sievers, Wm., barkeeper, 41½ Calumet ave; res 41 Calumet ave.
Simons, D. E., stock farm, south of city; res 75 N. Washington.
Skinner, D. F., Pres't First Nat'l Bank; res 56 N. Washington & Erie.
Skinner, Ed. H., clerk, res 8 E Mechanic.
Skinner, Fred., marble polisher; res 53 S Washington.
Skinner, J. Hanford, cashier, State Bank Valparaiso; res 86 E Erie.
Skinner, Leslie R , clerk; res 56 N Washington.
Skinner, Morgan C., res 53 S Washington.
Skinner, Saml. S., banker; res 53 S Washington.
Skinner, Miss Susie, principal High School; res 60 S Franklin.
Skinner, T. H., carpenter; res 33 N Napoleon.
Slover, Miss Harriet, res 108 E Main.
Slover, Mrs. Rebecca, 108 E Main.
SMALL, E. ELDENE, Journalist; res 25 N Franklin.
Small, Elwood E , correspondent *Star;* res 41 N Franklin.

Small, Mrs. Mary A., boarding; res 41 N Franklin.
SMITH, A. C., Druggist, 3 S Franklin; res 35 Jefferson and Michigan.
Smith, Benj. F., mail clerk Val. P. O.; 77 E Main.
Smith, Miss Bertha E., clerk; res 77 E Main.
Smith, David J., bridge carpenter; res 47 N Michigan.
Smith, Dr. John L. D. D.; res 70 E Chicago.
Smith, Rev. J. H. O , pastor Christian Church; res 39 N Morgan.
Smith, James, hackdriver; res 58 S Franklin.
Smith, Hudson F.; res 97 N Franklin.
Smith, Mrs. L. G.; res 67 N Washington.
Smith, Ora W., Cornell & Smith; res 9 N Academy.
Smith, Mrs. Mary E., dressmaker: boards Grand Central Hotel.
Smith, Mrs. Sylvester W.; res 77 E Main.
Smith, Wm. A., carpenter; res 4 Pearl.
Smutzer, Edward F., butcher, Washington; res 50 N Franklin.
Smutzer, Frank, butcher, Washington; res 90 E Main.
Snyder, James A , hedge trimmer; res 64 S Franklin.
Sowers, Frank, teamster; res 16 S Washington.
Sowers, John H., laborer; res 68 W Mechanic.
Sowers, Sanford, laborer; res 68 W Mechanic.
Sowers, Mrs. Theresa; res 69 W. Mechanic.
Sonnenberg, Gottlieb, tailor; res 67 S Washington.
Sonnenberg, Miss Lena, clerk, with E. Schneider; res 49 S Washington.
Southworth, A. A.; Lapanta ave.
Spath, John; res 17 Pearl.
Spath, John J., carpenter; res 17 Pearl.
Spath, Louis, section hand G. T. R. R.; res 17 Pearl.
Specht & Finney, gent's furnishings, 59 College ave.
Specht, Claus, Specht & Finney; res 38 N Michigan.
Spohn, U. G., rooms; res 47 S Locust.
Spooner, W. F., grocery, cor Main and Napoleon; res 9 N Campbell.
Sprencel, Frank, laborer; res 66 W Jefferson.
Sprencel, Louis, bridge carpenter; res 13 N Campbell.
Sprencel, Mrs. T.; res 66 W Jefferson.
Stabler, Rev. Henry, pastor St. Johns German Evangelical Church; res 71 E Jefferson.
Stalbaunn, Jocie, domestic; boards 6 Calumet ave.
Standahl. Chas., tailor; res 8 S Campbell.
Stanley, Raymond; res 23 West.
Stanton, Geo. E., J. Lowenstine; res n w cor Institute and Franklin.
Stanton, James, clerk.
State Bank of Valparaiso, banking, 14 E Mechanic.
Starr, A. E., Deputy Treas.; res 59 N Lafayette.
Starr, Decatur A.; res 65 N Washington.

Starr, Elmer E., jeweler, 1 E Main; res 59 N Lafayette.
Stauffer, Mrs. Peter; res 60 E Monroe.
Steele, Chas.; bds 34 N East
Stemer, Miss Emma, domestic; bds cor E Chicago and N Morgan.
Stephens, Mrs. C. J.; res 59 N Washington.
Stephens, O. S., carpenter; res 47 N Napoleon.
Stephens, James; res 141 E Main.
Stephens, Melvin M., clerk; res 47 N Napoleon.
Steppel, A. W., barber, Central House; res 28 Lafayette.
Stevens, George, section hand; res 2 E Water.
Steward, Miss, milliner; res 40 E Mechanic.
Steward, Mrs. Eliza J.; res 2 Union.
Steward, Harry P., teacher; res 2 Union.
Stick, John; res 21 West.
Stindahl, Chas., tailor, J. W. McNay; res Academy.
Stokes, Thos., engineer, Ft. Wayne Ry; res 15 E Monroe.
Stoner, Charles, saw mill, Grand Trunk depot; res 45 E Main.
Stoner, Mrs. Elizabeth; res 28 S Locust.
Stoner, Jacob; res 26 S Locust.
Stoner, Russell, W. J. Henry & Co.; res 27 S Locust.
Stoops, Mrs. M., boarding; res 51 S College.
Stolt, Mrs. Lizzie.
Stotterman, T., butcher; res 36 W Monroe.
Storr, Edward, wrks Ryan's livery; res 15 S. Franklin.
Stratton, John W., prop'r and m'g'r Valparaiso G. &. T St. Co.; res 51 W Jefferson.
Stratton, Henry, clerk C & G T Ry; res E Chicago cor Franklin.
Struve, Peter, laborer; res 26 West.
Stuckman, Edwin D., teacher; res 59 S Morgan.
Stuckman, Mrs. Emma, teacher; res 59 S Morgan.
Stuckman, Geo. W., teacher; res 59 S Morgan.
Stuckman, Henry, real estate, Monon; res 78 College ave.
Stuckman, Wm. M., teacher; 59 S Morgan.
Studer, Wilson S., conductor, P & F W Ry; res 83 N Franklin.
Sullivan, James, messenger; res 53 N Napoleon.
Sullivan, John H., showman; res 66 E Erie.
Sullivan, John, blacksmith helper; res 53 E Elm.
Sullivan, Marion; res 17 N Academy.
Sullivan, Mike; res West.
Suman, Frank, waiter; res 22 La Porte ave.
Suman, Col. I C. B., farmer; res 22 La Porte ave.
Summer, John, engineer, plaining mill; res 76 E Erie.
Summer, S. J., confectionery store, 11 N Washington; res 56 W Main.
Summers, John, engineer; res S E College ave & Institute.
Summers, S. J., confectioner; res 58 W Main.
Surgeon, Melvin, candy store, Main; res 7 Western ave.
Surgeon, Will, candy store, Main; res 7 Western ave.

Surgeon, Wm., city marshal; res 7 Western ave.
Swartout, A. D., contractor bldg, Greyson's Rest; res 11 S East.
Swartz, Wm., barber, Central House bldg.
Swartzkopf, Christopher, shoemaker, Ellsworth; res 34 E Monroe.
Sevenor, Nelson; res 16 South.
Taber, David F., sign painter, res 85 N Washington.
Tabor, James, res 47 E Chicago.
Talbert, W. J., Dalson & Talbert, res 33 South Jefferson.
Talcott, Jos. F., boots and shoes, 9 E Main.
Talcott, Wm. C., editor Vidette, res E Water.
Talbott, Adrian L., res 12 E Chicago.
Talbott, W. Irving, Dolson & Talbott, res 54 S Franklin.
Taylor, Howard H., works clock factory, res 32 E Monroe.
Teats, Jacob N., res 44 S Locust.
Templeton, —, res 147 S Greenwich.
Terrill, Walter, teamster, res 70 W Mechanic.
Tetzleff, Augusta, domestic, bds 70 N Washington.
Thatcher, John, clerk, res N Napoleon.
Thatcher, Miss Jennie V., teacher, res 84 E Jefferson.
Thatcher, Sam'l J., traveling salesman, res 84 E Jefferson.
Thedens, Annie, domestic, res 45 N Lafayette.
Thedens, Geo., works planing mill, res College Hill.
Thedens, Gurgen, carpenter, res 13 E Union.
Thiesen, Claus, res 44 Greenwich.
Thim, Hans F., drayman, res 79 N Napoleon.
Timming, Rudolph, res 41 E Chicago.
Thomas, Elias, internal rev. inspector, res 91 N Washington.
Thomas, Miss Nervie, domestic, bds 5 E Elm.
Thompson, Alfred M., engineer, res 13 E Elm.
Thompson, John, compositor, res Farmer's Hotel.
Thompson, Rev. John J., Pastor So Valpo M. E Church, res 81 E Main.
Thompson, Matthew M., carpenter, res 36 S Locust.
Thompson, Willard E., telegraph operator, res 81 E Main.
Thorsol, Chas., jewelry, 21 E Main, res cor Lafayette and Mechanic.
Thun, Albert, fireman, res 59 S Greenwich.
Thun, Albert, res 78 Union.
Thun, Henry, carpenter, res 78 Union.
Thun, Mrs. Mary, laundress, res 24 S Locust.
Thun, Willie, brakeman, G T. R. R., res 78 Union.
Thune, John, res 82 E Jefferson.
Tibbe, Tina, laundress, bds 106 N Washington.
Timm, Max H., mason, 15 S East.
Timmons, Henry J., saloon, W Main, res 72 E Erie.
Toering, Lizzie, domestic, res 83 N Washington.
Tofte, John, res 15 Haas.
Torry, R. G., res.10 S Lafayette.

Trahan, Israel, wagonmaker, res 3 S East.
Trahold, Miss Emma, domestic, res 74 N Washington.
Traver, Geo. P., res 34 Locust.
Traver, Raauf W., teacher, res 47 Institute.
Trudell, Edward, laborer, res 98 E Mechanic.
Trudell, Wilford, blacksmith, res 94 E Main.
Truman, J. W., merchant tailor, res 36 Morgan.
Truman, M. L., tailoress, res 36 Morgan.
Turner, David, carpenter, res 38 N Napoleon.
Turner, Frank A., real estate and insurance, 6 S Washington, res 55 S Washington.
Turner, Jas. W., postal clerk, res 26 E Chicago.
Turner, Mrs. Matthew, res 26 E Chicago.
Tuthill, Marrion E, painter, res Axe ave. & Nickel Plate R. R.
Tully, Miss Mary, seamstress, res Kinsey.
Tully, Wm., res 12 Kinzie.
Unger, Christian, teamster; res 32 S Napoleon.
Unruh, Fred, laborer; res 32 West.
Unruh, Mrs. Susan; res 72 S Morgan.
Unruh, Wm., res 12 N College ave.
UPTHEGROVE, H. J., Manufacturer Sportsmen's Clothing, 13 E Main; res 48 N Michigan.
Urbahns, John, saloon keeper, 3 W Mechanic; res 34 S Washington.
Urbahns, Mrs. T., res 13 Chestnut.
Urbahn, Robert, druggist, cor Main & Washington, res 13 Chestnut.
Van Horn, George P.; res 21 E Jefferson.
Van Ness, Elliott F., electrician; res 87 N Franklin.
Van Wagner, Wilmer, laborer; res 5 S Spring.
Van Wagner, Alfred, laborer; res 5 Spring.
Vannater, James A; res 87 N Lafayette.
Vail, W. H.; res 10 W Jefferson.
Valparaiso Gas & Electric Light Co., cor Napoleon & Water.
Valparaiso Lodge, K. P. 184, hall; 15 W Mechanic.
Valpo. Steam Laundry, H. B. Alberry, prop, cor Mechanic and Lafayette.
Vantrees, John, wagonmaker, W Main; res 55 N Napoleon.
Vastbinder, Ephraim, carpenter; res 72 E Erie.
Vastbinder, Mrs. E., dressmaker; res 72 E Erie.
Veach, H. Willard; res 15 E Water.
Vedstaid, Paul, grocer, 3 Washington; res 76 E Mechanic.
Vevia, Mrs. Florence; res 89 E Mechanic.
Vevia, Wm., barber; res 83 W Main.
VINCENT, A. W., M. D., Physician, 1 S Franklin; res 43 N Washington.
Volkee, E. C.; res 9 Cemetery ave.
Volkee. Ernesr F., rooms; res 52 S College ave.

THE VALPO
Steam ✳ Laundry
QUICK SERVICE.

WORK TURNED OUT IN 6 HOURS.   BEST WORK DONE IN THE CITY.

➣TRY US!➢

Finish polish or the plainest domestic finish. Lace Curtains, Pillow Shams and Ladies' Fine Fabrics a specialty. We do Family Washing. Goods called for and delivered.

Cor. Lafayette and Mechanic Streets,

H. B. ALBERY, Prop.   VALPARAISO, IND.

MODEL
News and Stationery Depot.

22 West Main Street
VALPARAISO, IND.

Subscriptions Received for Foreign and Domestic Publications.

Remember we are Headquarters for
FINE STATIONERY
AND ALL LATE NOVELTIES.

Agents for Chicago Morning and Evening Papers. Delivery made to any part of the city.

NORTHERN INDIANA
Law School

H. B. BROWN, President.

MARK L. DeMOTTE,
A. L. JONES, } Instructors.
H. A. GILLETT,

This School was organized in 1880 and has had a successful career. It has constantly increased in usefulness and numbers, and in its first decade has fully demonstrated the fact that

A THOROUGH LEGAL EDUCATION

can be secured at one-half the expense usually incurred in attending professional schools.

VALPARAISO, IND.

Von Doehren, John, butcher; res 6 N Locust.
Vroman, Frank A., night yard con., C & G T Ry; res 9 E Elm.
Vroman, James; res 9 E Elm.
Wade, Edw., laborer, res N Locust N of C. & G. T. Ry.
Wade, Geo. E., printer, res 23 S Greenwich.
Wade, Grant, bookbinder, res 77 S College ave.
Wager, Jacob H., res 26 College ave.
Wade, Jemmie A., res 42 Freeman.
Wade, Lewis, teamster, res 31 E Institute.
Wade, Mrs. Nellie. dressmaking, res 31 E Institute.
Wade, Otto, res N Locust, N of C. & G. T. Ry.
Wade, Walter G., barber, res 78 N Michigan.
Wagner, Anton, laborer, res 58 S Lafayette.
Wagner, Miss Gusta, domestic, res 47 N Washington.
Wagenroth, William, laborer, res Ore.
Wahl, Lena, dressmaker, res 73 N Morgan.
Walb, Mrs. Lucinda, res 42 S College ave.
Walker, James A, jeweler, 1 E Main, res 56 N Michigan.
Walkup, Thomas, works clock factory, res 40 E Jefferson.
Wallace, Geo. W., commercial traveler, res 12 S Napoleon.
Walsh, Mrs. M., seamstress, res 59 W Jefferson.
Ward, Thos., saloon, 12 W Main.
Warehouse, —, res 39 N Napoleon.
Wark, John, hides and leather, 6 E Mechanic, res 9 E Monroe.
Warner, Miss Eliza, res 26 College ave.
Warner, Miss May, teacher, res 42 E Erie.
Warner, Mrs. Mary, res 42 E Erie.
Wasser, Mrs. Hattie, rooms, res 97 E Mechanic.
Wasser, William B., bridge carpenter, res 97 E Mechanic.
Watt, W. M., drayman, res 96 Greenwich.
Weininger, Erillas, res 106 E Mechanic.
Weinkauf, Miss Annie, laundress, bds 106 N Washington.
Weinkauf, Miss Lizzie, laundress, bds 106 N Washington.
Weir, Ellsworth E., atty., res cor E Jefferson and N College ave.
Welch, John H, res 11 Factory.
Wells, George, day baggageman, C. & G. T. Ry., res 53 Calumet ave.
Wells, Guy M., clerk, res 57 E Monroe.
Wells, Paul I., clerk, res 57 E Monroe.
Wells, R. P., res Union Place.
Wells, Wm., res 49 E Jefferson.
Wells, Wm. C., res 57 E Monroe.
Welty, Edward, editor Vidette, res 71 N Lafayette.
Wenk, Franklin S., works clock factory, res 42 W Chicago.
Wendt, J. D., agent N. Y. C. & St. L. Ry., res 12 S Water.
Wandt, V. Henry, agent Nickel Plate, res 18 E Water.
Wesner, Jacob J., rooms, res 39 E Water.
Wessendorf, Fritz, works P. F. W. & C. Ry., res 4 West.

Westphal, John, res 11 S Greenwich.
Wetzler, Martin, teamster, res 118 W Main.
Weyer, Anthony, res 123 E Main.
Wheeler, A. S., works DuLaney clock fac'y, res 62 E Chicago.
Wheeler, Dudley D., carpenter, res 10 E Chicago.
Wheeler, G., broom maker, 108 W Main.
Wheeler, Leon E., res 62 E Chicago.
Wheeler, Roy S , works DuLaney clock fac'y, res 62 E Chicago.
Whitcomb, E. L., justice of the peace, 18 S Washington, res 57 Calumet ave.
Whitcomb, Miss Kate B., dressmaker, with Mrs. Pennock, res 57 Calumet ave.
White, Elmer, Heineman & White, res 49 N Michigan.
White, L. T., carpenter, res 25 East.
White, Mrs. T. C., White, McFetrich & Co., res 73 W Main.
White, McFetrich & Co., lumber, shingle, sash, etc., 80 W Mechanic.
Whitehead, Ed, works planing mill, res west of Valpo.
Wick, John, McClellan lumber yard, res 9 Spring.
Wiedeman, John, res 17 W Monroe.
Wiese, Miss, rooms, res 77 S Locust.
Wilder, Wayne, operator, Western Union Tel., res —Franklin.
Williams, Geo., horse trader, 19 E Main.
Williams, Henry T., Barmco & Williams; res 44 N Napoleon.
Williams, Meribah, milliner, 19 E Main.
Williams, Miss Ethel, dressmaker: res 36 S Locust.
Willits, Eugen V., foreman *Daily Star;* res 29 N Lafayette.
Willoughby, John, policeman; res 131 E Main.
Wilscam, Chas., carpenter; res 25 N Academy.
Wilscam, Joseph, laborer; res 42 N Academy.
Wilscam, Mitchell, laborer; res 29 N Academy.
Wilscam, Wm., carpenter; res 29 N Academy.
Wilson & Cameron, tubular well goods, cor Valparaiso and Poplar.
Wilson, Edmund L., contractor; res 90 N Franklin.
Wilson, Geo., hardware, E Main; res 63 E Chicago.
Wilson, James W., plumber; res 42 N Washington.
Wilson, John D., contractor; res 90 N Franklin.
Wilson, John H., Wilson & Cameron; res 85 N Franklin.
Wilson, Mrs. Catherine; res 49 N Lafayette.
Wilson, Rev. J. H., Pres Elder Valparaiso Dis M. E. Church; res 66 E Chicago.
Wilson, Wm. L., hardware, Main; res 8 W Institute.
Wilson, W.; res 42 N Washington.
Winbegly, Miss Inez, domestic; bds 90 N Franklin.
Windle, Lemuel A., Windle & Pettit; res 59 N Michigan.
Windle & Pettit, blacksmith; res 11 S Michigan.
Windle, W. G., grocer and baker, s e cor Main and Franklin.

Wininger, Mrs. Lavinia, laundress; res 11 E Union.
Wininguth, Adolph C., shoemaker, 23 Union; res 9 La Porte ave.
Winnerstrom, rooms; res 63 Freeman.
Wise, Jesse L. B., compositor; res 83 S Locust.
Wise, Mrs. Eliza; res 83 S Locust.
Wise, Mrs. J. L. B., compositor; res 83 S Locust.
Winslow, Aaron F., county constable; res 5 S Locust.
Winslow, D. Franklin; res 104 E Mechanic.
Winslow, Isaac, farmer; res 81 E Mechanic.
Winslow, Mrs. Leora; res 74 E Erie.
Winslow, Moses F., carpenter; res 75 N Franklin.
Winters, J. P., att'y-at-law, 18 S Washington.
Witmak, Albert, brakeman, P. F. W. & C. Ry.; res 61 S Franklin.
Witmak, August, painter; res 61 S Franklin.
Witmak, Mrs. Sophie; res 61 S Franklin.
Wolfe, Richard P., agt. Chicago Suit & Pants Co.; res 10 E Mechanic.
Wolgamot, Mrs. L. W.; res 33 N Morgan.
WONG LET, DR., Physician; res 39 E Mechanic.
Wonser, Edmund E., laborer; res E Sefton Bldg.
Wood, May, domestic; res 64 N Michigan.
Wood, Oliver S., M. D.; res 41 S Franklin.
Woodhull, A. E.; res 31 N Campbell.
Woodruff, Dwight, clerk, Louderback's grocery; res 47 E Erie.
Woodward, C., works clock factory.
Wright, Effie; res 9 S East.
Wright, Miss Lizzie; res 61 W Main.
Wrenn, Pat'k. H., night yard brakeman, C. & G. T. Ry.; res Calumet ave.
Wright, Prof. Saml. B., Art Dept. Ind. State Normal; res 19 S Greenwich.
Wulff, Herman, harnessmaker, 6 E Mechanic; res 80 E Main.
Yager, Maggie, domestic; res 25 N Napoleon.
Yahn, J. F., barber; res 64 E Chicago.
Young, Artemes, clerk; res 111 N Washington.
Young, Joseph H.; res 40 E Mechanic.
Young, W. Clark, farmer; res 75 E Jefferson.
Young, Wm., clerk; res Water.
Younglove, Dan'l, yard conductor C & G T Ry; res 83 N Morgan.
Younglove, Mrs. Mary E.; res 35 N Franklin.
Younglove, H., bartender, Daily & Reagan.
Youngs, Wm. N., foreman Bell's livery, 58 E Mechanic; res 14 E Water.
Youngjohann, Henry; res 5 Union.
Yutter, Geo. F., barber; res 41 Michigan.
Zee, Joseph; res 71 N Morgan.
Zimmerman, Albert L., mach., Kellogg Mfg Co.; res 49 W Main.

Zimmerman, Andrew J., engraver; res 31 N Washington.
Zimmerman, Arthur F., manager *The Sun*, bds 33 W Mechanic.
Zimmerman, E., editor and proprietor the *Messenger* and *Sun;* res 49 W Main.
Zimmerman, Miss Julia, medicines; res 15 W Jefferson.
Zook, D. Coder, foreman F W Ry; res 64 E Mechanic.
Zorn, —; 31 S Morgan.

www.ingramcontent.com/pod-product-compliance
Lightning Source LLC
Chambersburg PA
CBHW030405170426
43202CB00010B/1499